SAMUEL L. CLEMENS

AMERICAN PORTRAITS

1875–1900

BY

GAMALIEL BRADFORD

With Illustrations

KENNIKAT PRESS/PORT WASHINGTON, N. Y.

AMERICAN PORTRAITS: 1875-1900

Copyright 1922 by Gamaliel Bradford
Reissued in 1969 by Kennikat Press by arrangement with
Houghton Mifflin Company
Library of Congress Catalog Card No: 71-85994
SBN 8046-0539-4

Manufactured by Taylor Publishing Company   Dallas, Texas

ESSAY AND GENERAL LITERATURE INDEX REPRINT SERIES

TO

GARLAND GREEVER

BERNADILLE

C'est ce que l'on appelle le cœur humain.

MARGOT

Le cœur humain?

BERNADILLE

Ça ne devrait pas être comme ça, et c'est comme ça.

COQUEBERT

Le philosophe s'en étonne.

BERNADILLE

Le moraliste s'en afflige — il s'en afflige, le moraliste! mais c'est tout de même comme ça.

MEILHAC AND HALÈVY

PREFACE

THIS group of portraits is the first of a series in which I hope to cover American history, proceeding backwards with four volumes on the nineteenth century, two on the eighteenth, and one on the seventeenth. My intention is to include representative figures in all the varied lines of life, statesmen and men of action, writers, artists, preachers, scholars, professional men, and men prominent in the business world. Among the numerous difficulties of such an undertaking, not the least is that of entering into the special achievements of all these distinguished persons. To judge what they accomplished, it would be necessary to be expert in their different pursuits. But I am concerned with their souls and deal with their work only as their souls are illustrated in it.

I am aware that in the present volume I have not carried out my aim so fully as I could wish. There are too many writers and artists. Blaine and Cleveland go far to restore the balance with practical life. And among the literary and artistic figures there is an ample variety and richness of contrast. But I should like to have included a man of pure science, and especially one of the men of large business capacity who are so typically American. What has balked me has been the difficulty of obtaining satisfactory material. With literary men such material is always abundant. Politicians have plenty of friends — or enemies — to record their experiences, if they do not do it themselves.

PREFACE

But the man of science is apt to be expressed wholly in his scientific investigation, and the man of business lives his work and does not write it. I hope, however, to return at a later period to the closing years of the nineteenth century and develop some of the striking figures who have teased my curiosity without satisfying it.

There are two drawbacks to any successful portrayal of one's contemporaries. The first is that it is peculiarly difficult to clear one's impression of prejudice. One can survey great persons of a hundred years ago with a fair amount of detachment from partisan views and personal sympathies. But men we have known, or whose friends we have known, come before us with a cloud of secondary associations which tend to confuse the fundamental spiritual issues. We are inclined to please somebody, or to spare somebody, or to annoy somebody. Even the coolest and most impartial find it hard to escape such influences. Sainte-Beuve himself, so broad and moderate in dealing with the seventeenth and eighteenth centuries, is obviously unjust and unreasonable with many of the great writers of his own day.

Again, the study of contemporaries is complicated by the constant appearance of new material. One examines every existing document with the utmost care and, alas, makes up one's mind. Then new records, new letters, new analyses, are published, and one has to unmake it, or reconsider the making, and one is never sure that one is doing it fairly. To take a striking instance. My portrait of Mark Twain was completed

PREFACE

before I read Mr. Van Wyck Brooks's "Ordeal of
Mark Twain." I endeavored to master Mr. Brooks's
point of view. It seemed to me that I did so, and that,
while I recognized its brilliancy and ingenuity, it did
not essentially affect my own original conception. But
I shall never be sure that, if I had read Mr. Brooks
first, my portrait would not have been different — and
better.

Another experience of this nature has occurred with
Henry Adams. My study, founded on the "Education" and the various works published by Adams
himself, was completed before the appearance of the
"Letters to a Niece" and the "Cycle of Adams Letters." The introduction to the former book suggested
some important modifications. But in this case it was
most interesting to find the main lines of the portrait
confirmed in the striking series of letters exchanged
between the Adamses, father and sons. What more is
needed to show the identity of the Henry Adams of
the Civil War and the Henry Adams of the "Education" than this passage, addressed to him by his elder
brother in 1862: "You set up for a philosopher. You
write letters *à la* Horace Walpole; you talk of loafing
round Europe; you pretend to have seen life. Such
twaddle makes me feel like a giant Warrington talking
to an infant Pendennis. *You* 'tired of this life'! *You*
more and more 'callous and indifferent about your own
fortunes'!... Fortune has done nothing but favor
you and yet you are 'tired of this life.' You are beaten
back everywhere before you are twenty-four, and
finally writing philosophical letters you grumble at the

strange madness of the times and haven't faith in God
and the spirit of your age. What do you mean by
thinking, much less writing such stuff?" (*Cycle*, vol I,
p. 102.) To which, for completeness, we may add these
words of Henry himself: "A man whose mind is bal-
anced like mine, in such a way that what is evil never
seems unmixed with good, and what is good always
streaked with evil; an object seems never important
enough to call out strong energies till they are exhausted, nor necessary enough not to allow of its
failure being possible." (*Cycle*, vol. I, p. 195.)

To the complications which peculiarly affect work
on contemporaries must be joined an increasing sense
of the difficulty of accomplishing the portrayal of souls
at all. More than ever I feel that such portrayal, at
least as I can perform it, has no final value. Souls
tremble and shift and fade under the touch. They
elude and evade and mock you, fool you with false
lights and perplex you with impenetrable shadows, till
you are almost ready to give up in despair any effort to
interpret them. But you cannot give it up; for there is
no artistic effort more fascinating and no study so
completely inexhaustible.

If the substance on which we have to found spiritual
interpretation could be relied on, we might have more
confidence in the superstructure. But the further we
go, the more our confidence is shaken. Take one special
form of material, the report of words and conversations.
All historians and biographers use such report, are
tempted to use it much more than they do. Yet how
abominably uncertain it is and must be. Who of us

PREFACE

can remember for an hour the exact words he himself used, even important words, significant words? Much more, who can remember such words of any one else? Yet diarists and biographers will go home and set down at the end of a long evening, or perhaps a day or two later, elaborate phrases which the alleged speaker may have used, and much more likely may not. And this, when the turn of a sentence may alter the light on a man's soul! Of such materials is biography made. I should not wish any one to have more confidence in mine, at least, than I have myself.

I desire to acknowledge generally the courtesy and helpfulness of many correspondents who have offered useful suggestions and corrected errors. And for the opportunity of profiting by these, I must chiefly thank the editor of the *Atlantic Monthly* whose steady and cordial support and sympathy enable me to prosecute my work with an enthusiasm which I could hardly draw from any other source.

GAMALIEL BRADFORD

WELLESLEY HILLS, MASSACHUSETTS
January, 1922

CONTENTS

ILLUSTRATIONS

AMERICAN PORTRAITS
1875–1900
I
MARK TWAIN

CHRONOLOGY

Samuel Langhorne Clemens.
Born, Florida, Missouri, November 30, 1835.
Pilot on the Mississippi, 1857–1861.
In the West, 1861–1866.
Innocents Abroad published, 1869.
Married Olivia Langdon, February 2, 1870.
Roughing It published, 1872.
Adventures of Tom Sawyer published, 1876.
Adventures of Huckleberry Finn published, 1884.
Failure of Webster & Company, 1894.
Wife died, June 5, 1904.
Degree of Doctor of Letters from Oxford, 1907.
Died, Redding, Connecticut, April 21, 1910.

AMERICAN PORTRAITS

I

MARK TWAIN

I

WHEN I was a boy of fourteen, Mark Twain took hold of me as no other book had then and few have since. I lay on the rug before the fire in the long winter evenings and my father read me "The Innocents Abroad" and "Roughing It" and "Old Times on the Mississippi," and I laughed till I cried. Nor was it all laughter. The criticism of life, strong and personal, if crude, the frank, vivid comments on men and things, set me thinking as I had never thought, and for several years colored my maturing reflection in a way that struck deep and lasted long.

Such is my youthful memory of Mark. For forty years I read little of him. Now, leaping over that considerable gulf, reading and re-reading old and new together, to distil the essence of his soul in a brief portrait, has been for me a wild revel, a riot of laughter and criticism and prejudice and anti-prejudice and revolt and rapture, from which it seems as if no sane and reasoned judgment could ensue. Perhaps none has.

This much is clear, to start with, that Mark is not to be defined or judged by the ordinary standards of mere writers or literary men. He was something different,

3

perhaps something bigger and deeper and more human, at any rate something different. He did a vast amount of literary work and did it, if one may say so, in a literary manner. He was capable of long, steady toil at the desk. He wrote and rewrote, revised his copy over and over again with patience and industry. He had the writer's sense of living for the public, too, instinctively made copy of his deepest personal emotions and experiences. One of his most striking productions is the account of the death of his daughter, Jean; but no one but a born writer would have deliberately set down such experiences at such a moment with publication in his thought. And he liked literary glory. To be sure, he sometimes denied this. In youth he wrote, "There is no satisfaction in the world's praise anyhow, and it has no worth to me save in the way of business." [1] Again, he says in age, "Indifferent to nearly everything but work. I like that; I enjoy it, and stick to it. I do it without purpose and without ambition; merely for the love of it." [2] All the same, fame was sweet to him.

Yet one cannot think of him as a professional writer. Rather, there is something of the bard about him, of the old, epic, popular singer, who gathered up in himself, almost unconsciously, the life and spirit of a whole nation and poured it forth, more as a voice, an instrument, than as a deliberate artist. Consider the mass of folk-lore in his best, his native books. Is it not just such material as we find in the spontaneous, elementary productions of an earlier age?

Better still, perhaps, we should speak of him as a

4

journalist; for a journalist he was essentially and always, in his themes, in his gorgeous and unfailing rhetoric, even in his attitude toward life. The journalist, when inspired and touched with genius, is the nearest equivalent of the old epic singer, most embodies the ideal of pouring out the life of his day and surroundings with as little intrusion as possible of his own personal, reflective consciousness.

And as Mark had the temperament to do this, so he had the training. No man ever sprang more thoroughly from the people or was better qualified to interpret the people. Consider the nomadic irrelevance of his early days, before his position was established, if it was ever established. Born in the Middle West toward the middle of the century, he came into a moving world, and he never ceased to be a moving spirit and to move everybody about him. He tried printing as a business, but any indoor business was too tame, even though diversified by his thousand comic inventions. Piloting on the vast meanders of the Mississippi was better. What contacts he had there, with good and evil, with joy and sorrow! But even the Mississippi was not vast enough for his uneasy soul. He roved the Far West, tramped, traveled, mined, and speculated, was rich one day and miserably poor the next; and all the time he cursed and jested alternately and filled others with laughter and amazement and affection and passed into and out of their lives, like the shifting shadow of a dream. Surely the line of the old poet was made for him,

"Now clothed in feathers he on steeples walks."

5

And thus it was that he met his friend's challenge to walk the city roofs, where they promenaded arm in arm, until a policeman threatened to shoot, and was only restrained by the explanatory outcry, "Don't shoot! That's Mark Twain and Artemus Ward." [3]

This was his outer youthful life, and within it was the same. For with some the feet wander while the soul sits still. It was not so with him. Though all his life he scolded himself for laziness, complained of his indolence, or gloried in it; yet when he was interested in anything, his heart was one mad fury of energy. Listen to his theory on the subject: "If I were a heathen, I would rear a statue to Energy, and fall down and worship it! I want a man to — I want *you* to — take up a line of action, and *follow* it out, in spite of the very devil." [4] And practice for himself never fell short of theory for others.

To be sure, his energy was too often at the mercy of impulse. Where his fancies led him, there he followed, with every ounce of force he had at the moment. What might come afterwards he did not stop to think about —until afterwards. Then there were sometimes bitter regrets, which did not prevent a repetition of the process. He touches off the whole matter with his unfailing humor: "I still do the thing commanded by Circumstance and Temperament, and reflect afterward. Always violently. When I am reflecting on these occasions, even deaf persons can hear me think." [5]

Perhaps the most amusing of all these spiritual efforts and adventures of his youth were his dealings with money. He was no born lover of money, and he was certainly no miser; but he liked what money brings, and from his childhood he hated debt and would not tolerate it. Therefore he was early and always on the lookout for sources of gain and was often shrewd in profiting by them. But what he loved most of all was to take a chance. His sage advice on the matter is: "There are two times in a man's life when he should not speculate: when he can't afford it and when he can." [6] Apparently his own life escaped from these all-embracing conditions; for he speculated always. A gold mine or a patent, an old farm or a new printing machine — all were alike to him, vast regions of splendid and unexplored possibility. And much as he reveled in the realities of life, possibility was his natural domain, gorgeous dreams and sunlit fancies, strange realms of the imagination, where his youthful spirit loved to wander and shape cloud futures that could never come to pass, as he himself well knew, and knew that to their unrealizable remoteness they owed the whole of their charm.

But, you say, this was, after all, youthful. When years came upon him, when he had tasted the sedate soberness of life, dreams must have grown dim or been forgotten. Far from it. His lovely wife called him "Youth," till she died, and he deserved it. Though he was married and a great author and had a dozen homes, he never settled down, neither his feet nor his soul. The spirit of his early ideal, "A life of don't-care-a-damn in a boarding-house is what I have asked for in many a secret prayer," [7] lingered with him always. You see, he had restless nerves, to which long quiet and solitary, sombre reflection were a horror. And then he had perfect, magnificent health, the kind that can endure boarding-houses without ruin. "In no other human being have I ever seen such physical endurance," says his biographer.[8] And Mark himself declared that he never knew what fatigue was. Who that was made like this would not be glad to wander forever? So Mark was most happy and most at home when he was wandering.

He saw and liked to see all things and all men and women. The touch of a human hand was pleasant to him, and the sound of a human voice, speaking no matter what lingo. He made friends of pilots and pirates and miners and peasants and emperors and clergymen, particularly clergymen, over whom he apparently exercised such witchery that oaths from him fell on their ears like prayers from other people. No man ever more abused the human heart, or railed more at the hollowness of human affection, and no man ever had more friends or loved more. To be sure, he could hate, with humorous frenzy and apparently with persistence. But love in the main prevailed and, indeed, what anchored his wandering footsteps was not places but souls, was love and tenderness. He had plenty for the pilots and the pirates and the clergymen. He had much more for those who were nearest him. His infinite devotion to his daughters, most of all to his wife, who was fully worthy of it and who understood and brought out the best in him and tolerated what was not so good, is not the least among the things that make him lovable.

As he was a creature of contradictions, it is no surprise to find that, while he prayed for boarding-houses, he loved comfort and even luxury. He would have eaten off a plank in a mining-camp, and slept on one; but the softest beds and the richest tables were never unwelcome, and one attraction of wandering was to see how comfortable men can be as well as how uncomfortable. Now, to have luxury, you must have money. And Mark, in age as in youth, always wanted money, whether from mines in Nevada, or from huge books sold by huge subscription, or from strange and surprising inventions that were bound to revolutionize the world and bring in multimillions. He always wanted money, though rivers of it ran in to him — and ran out again. He spent it, he gave it away, he never had it, he always wanted it.

And always, till death, his soul wandered even more than his body did. And his adventures with money were mainly matters of dream, even when the dreams were punctuated with sharp material bumps. Again and again some exciting speculation appealed to him, as much for its excitement as for its profit. He built great cloud castles and wandered in them and bade his friends admire them and made colossal calculations of enormous successes. Then the clouds collapsed and vanished and the flaw in the calculations became apparent — too late. Calculations were never a strong point with him, whether of assets or liabilities. He spent a white night working over the latter: "When I came down in the morning a gray and aged wreck, and went over the figures again, I found that in some

9

unaccountable way I had multiplied the totals by 2. By God, I dropped 75 years on the floor where I stood." [9]

Even his loves had an element of dream in them, and surely dream made up a large portion of his hatred. Certain natures offended him, exasperated him, and he amused himself with furious assertion of how he would like to torment them. If he had seen one of them suffer, even in a finger's end, he would have done all in his power to relieve it. But in the abstract how he did luxuriate in abuse of these imaginary enemies, what splendor of new-coined damnation he lavished on them, and all a matter of dreams!

Something of dream entered also into his widespread glory; for such wealth of praise and admiration has surely not often fallen upon walkers of the firm-set earth. During the first decade of the twentieth century he drifted in his white dream garments — as Emily Dickinson did in solitude — through dream crowds who applauded him and looked up to him and loved him. And he ridiculed it, turned it inside out to show the full dream lining, and enjoyed it, enjoyed his vast successes on the public platform, enjoyed the thronging tributes of epistolary admirers, enjoyed the many hands that touched his in loving and grateful tenderness.

And at the end, to make the dream complete, as if it were the conception of a poet, a full, rounded, perfect tragedy, misfortunes and disasters piled in upon the dream glory and thwarted and blighted it, even while their depth of gloom seemed to make its splendor more imposing. Money, which had all along seduced him, betrayed him, for a time at any rate, and he wallowed in the distress of bankruptcy, till he made his own shoulders lift the burden. One of his daughters, who was very dear to him, died when he was far away from her. His wife died and took happiness with her and made all glory seem like sordid folly. His youngest daughter died suddenly, tragically. What was there left?

Nothing. Toys, trifles, snatched moments of oblivion, billiards, billiards, till midnight, then a little troubled sleep, and more billiards till the end. In perhaps the most beautiful words he ever wrote he summed up the fading quality of it all under this very figure of a dream: "Old Age, white-headed, the temple empty, the idols broken, the worshipers in their graves, nothing but You, a remnant, a tradition, belated fag-end of a foolish dream, a dream that was so ingeniously dreamed that it seemed real all the time; nothing left but You, centre of a snowy desolation, perched on the ice-summit, gazing out over the stages of that long *trek* and asking Yourself, 'Would you do it again if you had the chance?'" [10]

II

MARK TWAIN is generally known to the world as a laugher. His seriousness, his pathos, his romance, his instinct for adventure, are all acknowledged and enjoyed. Still, the mention of his name almost always brings a smile first. So did the sight of him.

There is no doubt that he found the universe laughable and made it so. The ultimate test of the laughing instinct is that a man should be always ready to laugh at himself. Mark was. The strange chances of his life, its ups and downs, its pitiful disasters, sometimes made him weep, often made him swear. But at a touch they could always make him laugh. "There were few things that did not amuse him," writes his biographer, "and certainly nothing amused more, or oftener, than himself." [11] One brief sentence sums up what he was never tired of repeating, "I have been an author for 20 years and an ass for 55." [12] And he not only saw laughter when it came to him. He went to seek it. He was always fond of jests and fantastic tricks, made mirth out of solemn things and solemn people, stood ready, like the clown of the circus, to crack his whip and bid the world dance after him in quaint freaks of jollity, all the more diverting when staid souls and mirthless visages played a chief part in the furious revel.

On the strength of this constant sense and love of laughter many have maintained that Mark was one of the great world humorists, that he ranks with Cervantes and Sterne and the Shakespeare of "As You Like It" and "Twelfth Night," as one who was an essential exponent of the comic spirit. With this view I cannot wholly agree. It is true that Mark could find the laughable element in everything, true also that he had that keen sense of melancholy which is inseparable from the richest comedy. Few have expressed this more intensely than he has: "Everything human is pathetic. The secret source of humor itself is not joy,

12

but sorrow. There is no humor in heaven." [13] Yet the very extravagance of expression here suggests my difficulty. Somehow in Mark the humor and the pathos are not essentially blended. The laughter is wild and exuberant as heart can desire. But it does not really go to the bottom of things. Serious matters, so-called serious matters, are taken too seriously; and under the laughter there is a haunting basis of wrath and bitterness and despair.

To elucidate this it is necessary to examine and follow the process and progress of Mark's thinking. In early years, as he himself admits, he thought little, that is, abstractly. His mind was active enough, busy enough, and, as we have seen, his fancy was always full of dreams. But he let the great problems alone, did not analyze, did not philosophize, content to extract immense joviality from the careless surface of life and not probe further. Even the analysis of laughter itself did not tempt him. In this he was probably wise and he maintained the attitude always. "Humor is a subject which has never had much interest for me." [14] Indeed, the analysis of humor may be safely left to those gray persons who do not know what it is. But much of the jesting of Mark's youthful days is so trivial that it distinctly implies the absence of steady thinking on any subject. Not that he was indifferent to practical seriousness. Wrong, injustice, cruelty, could always set him on fire in a moment. There was no folly about his treatment of these. But at that stage his seriousness was busy with effects rather than with causes.

Then he acquired money and leisure and began to

reflect upon the nature of things. This late dawning of his speculative turn must always be remembered in considering the quality of it. It accounts for the singular gaps in his information about simple matters, for the impression of terrific but not very well-guided energy which comes from his intellectual effort. It accounts for the sense of surprise and novelty in his spiritual attitude, which Howells so justly pointed out. [15] He seems always like a man discovering things which are perfectly well known to trained thinkers, and this gives an extraordinary freshness and spirit to his pronouncements on all speculative topics.

When he became aware of his reasoning powers, he delighted in them. His shrewd little daughter said of him, "He is as much of a philosopher as anything, I think." [16] He was a philosopher by inclination, at any rate. He loved to worry the universe, as a kitten worries a ball of yarn. Perhaps this seemed to make up in a small way for the worries the universe had given him. He loved to argue and discuss and dispute and confute, and then to spread over all bitterness the charm of his inextinguishable laughter. His oaths and jests and epigrams convulsed his interlocutors, if they did not convince them.

As to his theoretical conclusions, it may be said that they were in the main nihilistic. But before considering them more particularly, it must be insisted and emphasized that they were theoretical and did not affect his practical morals. Few human beings ever lived who had a nicer conscience and a finer and more delicate fulfilment of duty. It is true that all his life he kept up a constant humorous depreciation of himself in this regard. If you listened to his own confessions, you would think him the greatest liar in existence and conclude that his moral depravation was only equaled by his intellectual nullity. This method is often effective for hiding and excusing small defects and delinquencies. But Mark needed no such excuse. What failings there were in his moral character were those incident to humanity. As an individual he stood with the best.

The most obvious instances of his rectitude are in regard to money. In spite of his dreams and speculative vagaries, he was punctiliously scrupulous in financial relations, his strictness culminating in the vast effort of patience and self-denial necessary to pay off the debt of honor which fell upon him in his later years. But the niceness of his conscience was not limited to broad obligations of this kind. "Mine was a trained Presbyterian conscience," he says, "and knew but the one duty — to hunt and harry its slave upon all pretexts and all occasions." [17] He might trifle, he might quibble, he might jest; but no one was more anxious to do what was fair and right, even to the point of overdoing it. "I don't wish even to *seem* to do anything which can invite suspicion," he said, as to a matter so trivial as taking advantage in a game. [18]

And the moral sense was not confined to practical matters of conduct. Human tenderness and kindliness and sympathy have rarely been more highly developed than in this man who questioned their existence. The finest touch in all his writings is the cry of Huck Finn

15

when, after a passionate struggle between his duty to society and his duty to friendship, he tears the paper in which he proposed to surrender the nigger, Jim, and exclaims, "All right, then, I'll *go* to hell." [19] And Mark himself would have been perfectly capable, not only of saying he would go, but of going.

As he loved men,'so he trusted them. In the abstract, judging from himself, he declared they were monsters of selfishness, greedy, deceitful, treacherous, thoughtful in all things of their own profit and advantage. In the individual, again judging from himself, he accepted them at their face value, as kindly, self-sacrificing, ready to believe, ready to love, ready to help. Being himself an extreme example, both in sceptical analysis and in human instinct, he often fell into error and trusted where there was no foundation to build on.

In consequence his actual experience went far to justify his sceptical theories, and he presents another instance, like Byron, like Leopardi, of a man whose standard of life is so high, who expects so much of himself and of others, that the reality perpetually fails him, and excess of optimism drives him to excess of pessimism. For example, his interesting idealization or idolatry of Joan of Arc, his belief that she actually existed as a miracle of nature, makes it comprehensible that he should find ordinary men and women faulty and contemptible enough compared with such a type.

It is not the place here to analyze Mark's speculative conclusions in detail. They may be found theoretically elaborated in "What is Man?", practically applied in "The Mysterious Stranger" and the "Maxims of

Pudd'nhead Wilson," and artistically illustrated in "The Man Who Corrupted Hadleyburg" and innumerable other stories. They may be summed up as a soul-less and blasting development of crude evolutionary materialism, as manifested in the teachings of Robert Ingersoll. Man's freedom disappears, his morality becomes enlightened selfishness, his soul is dissipated into thin air, his future life grows so dubious as to be disregarded, and the thought of death is only tolerable because life is not. The deity, in any sense of value to humanity, is quite disposed of; or, if he is left lurking in an odd corner of the universe, it is with such complete discredit that one can only remember the sarcasm of the witty Frenchman: "The highest compliment we can pay God is not to believe in him."

In all this perpetually recurrent fierce dissection of the divine and human, one is constantly impressed by the vigor and independence of the thinking. The man makes his own views; or since, as he himself repeatedly insists, no one does this, at least he makes them over, rethinks them, gives them a cast, a touch that stamps them Mark Twain's and no one else's, and, as such, significant for the study of his character, if for nothing more.

On the other hand, if the thinking is fresh and vigorous, one is also impressed and distressed by its narrowness and dogmatism. Here again the man's individuality shows in ample, humorous recognition of his own weakness, or excess of strength. No one has ever admitted with more delightful candor the encroaching passion of a preconceived theory. I have got a philosophy of life, he says, and the rest of my days will be spent in patching it up and "in looking the other way when an imploring argument or a damaging fact approaches." [20] Nevertheless, the impression of dogmatism remains, or, let us say better, of limitation. The thinking is acute, but it does not go to the bottom of things. The fundamental, dissolving influence of the idealistic philosophy, for instance, is not once suggested or comprehended. This shows nowhere more fully than in the discussion of Christian Science. Everything is shrewd, apt, brilliant, but wholly on the surface.

The effect of the bitter and withering character of Mark's thought on his own life was much emphasized by the lack of the great and sure spiritual resources that are an unfailing refuge to some of us. He could not transport himself into the past. When he attempted it, he carried all the battles and problems of to-day along with him, as in the "Yankee at the Court of King Arthur." He had not the historical feeling in its richest sense. Art, also, in all its deeper manifestations, was hidden from him. He could not acquire a love for classical painting or music, and revenged himself for his lack of such enjoyment by railing at those who had it. Even Nature did not touch great depths in him, because they were not there. He reveled in her more theatrical aspects, sunsets, ice-storms. Her energy stimulated a strange excitement in him, shown in Twitchell's account of his rapture over a mountain brook. [21] I do not find that he felt the charm of lonely walks in country solitude.

MARK TWAIN

It is on this lack of depth in thinking and feeling that I base my reluctance to class Mark with the greatest comic writers of the world. His thought was bitter because it was shallow; it did not go deep enough to get the humble tolerance, the vast self-distrust that should go with a dissolving vision of the foundations of the individual universe. His writing alternates from the violence of unmeaning laughter to the harshness of satire that has no laughter in it. In this he resembles Molière, whose Scapins are as far from reflection as are his Tartuffes from gayety. And Mark's place is rather with the bitter satirists, Molière, Ben Jonson, Swift, than with the great, broad, sunshiny laughers, Lamb, Cervantes, and the golden comedy of Shakespeare.

Indeed, no one word indicates better the lack I mean in Mark than "sunshine." You may praise his work in many ways; but could any one ever call it merry? He can give you at all times a riotous outburst of convulsing cachinnation. He cannot give you merriment, sunshine, pure and lasting joy. And these are always the enduring elements of the highest comedy.

III

But perhaps this is to consider too curiously. The vast and varied total of Mark's works affords other elements of interest besides the analysis of speculative thought, or even of laughter. Above all, we Americans should appreciate how thoroughly American he is. To be sure, in the huge mixture of stocks and races that surrounds us, it seems absurd to pick out anything or anybody as typically American. Yet we do it. We all choose Franklin as the American of the eighteenth century and Lincoln as the American of the nineteenth. And most will agree that Mark was as American as either of these.

He was American in appearance. The thin, agile, mobile figure, with its undulating ease in superficial awkwardness, suggested worlds of humorous sensibility. The subtle, wrinkled face, under its rich shock of hair, first red, then snowy white, had endless possibilities of sympathetic response. It was a face that expressed, repressed, impressed every variety of emotion known to its owner.

He was American in all his defects and limitations. The large tolerance, cut short with a most definite end when it reached the bounds of its comprehension, was eminently American. The slight flavor of vanity, at least of self-complacent satisfaction, the pleasant and open desire to fill a place in the world, whether by mounting a platform at just the right moment or wearing staring white clothes in public places, we may call American with slight emphasis, as well as human.

But these weaknesses were intimately associated with a very American excellence, the supreme candor, the laughing frankness which recognized them always. Assuredly no human being ever more abounded in such candor than Mark Twain. He confessed at all times, with the superabundance of diction that was born with him, all his enjoyment, all his suffering, all his sin, all his hope, all his despair.

And he was American in another delightful thing, his quickness and readiness of sympathy, his singular gentleness and tenderness. He could lash out with his tongue and tear anything and anybody to pieces. He could not have done bodily harm to a fly, unless a larger pity called for it. He was supremely modest and simple in his demands upon others, supremely depreciative of the many things he did for them. "I wonder why they all go to so much trouble for me. I never go to any trouble for anybody." [22] The quiet wistfulness of it, when you know him, brings tears.

Above all, he was American in his thorough democracy. He had a pitiful distrust of man; but his belief in men, all men, was as boundless as his love for them. Though he lived much with the rich and lofty, he was always perfectly at home with the simple and the poor, understood their thoughts, liked their ways, and made them feel that he had been simple and poor himself and might be so again.

He was not only democratic in feeling and spirit, he was democratic in authorship, both in theory and practice. Hundreds of authors have been obliged to write for the ignorant many, for the excellent reason that the cultivated few would not listen to them. Perhaps not one of these hundreds has so deliberately avowed his purpose of neglecting the few to address the many, as Mark did. The long letter to Mr. Andrew Lang, in which he proclaims this intention, is a curious document. Let others aim high, he says, let others exhaust themselves in restless and usually vain attempts to please fastidious critics. I write for the million, I want to please them, I know how to do it, I have done it. "I have never tried, in even one single

21

instance, to help cultivate the cultivated classes. . . .
I never had any ambition in that direction, but always
hunted for bigger game — the masses. I have seldom
deliberately tried to instruct them, but have done my
best to entertain them. To simply amuse them would
have satisfied my dearest ambition at any time." [23]

It is hardly necessary to dwell upon the weak points
in this theory. Whatever Mark, or any one else pro-
fesses, it cannot be questioned that he would prefer the
approbation of the cultured few, if he could get it.
Moreover, it may easily be maintained that the many
in most cases take their taste from the few; and if this
does not hold with a writer's contemporaries, it is
unfailing with posterity. If a writer is to please the
generations that follow him, he can do it only by secur-
ing the praise of those who by taste and cultivation are
qualified to judge. In other words, if Mark's works
endure, it will be because he appealed to the few as well
as to the many.

However this may be, there can be no question that
Mark reached the great democratic public of his own
day and held it. To be sure, it is doubtful whether even
he attained the full glory of what he and Stevenson
agreed to call submerged authorship, [24] the vast acceptance of those who are wept over at lone midnight by
the shop-girl and the serving-maid. But his best-
known books, "Tom Sawyer," "Huck Finn," "Life
on the Mississippi," "The Prince and the Pauper,"
may be justly said to belong to the literature of American democracy, and the travel books and many others
are not far behind these.

With this deliberate intention to appeal to the masses and to affect the masses, it becomes an essential part of the study of Mark's career and character to consider what his influence upon the masses was. He talked to them all his life, from the platform and from the printed page, with his sympathetic, human voice, his insinuating smile. What did his talk mean to them, how did it affect them, for good or for evil?

In the first place, beyond a doubt, enormously for good. Laughter in itself is an immense blessing to the weary soul, not a disputable blessing, like too much teaching and preaching, but a positive benefit. "Amusement is a good preparation for study and a good healer of fatigue after it," says Mark himself.[25] And amusement he provided, in vast abundance, muscle-easing, spirit-easing.

Also, he did more than make men laugh; he made them think, on practical, moral questions. He used his terrible weapon of satire to demolish meanness, greed, pettiness, dishonesty. He may have believed in the abstract that selfishness was the root of human action, but he scourged it in concrete cases with whips of scorpions. He may have believed in the abstract that men were unfit to govern themselves, but he threw the bitterest scorn on those who attempted to tyrannize over others.

Finally, Mark's admirers insist, and insist with justice, that he was a splendid agent in the overthrow of shams. He loved truth, sincerity, the simple recognition of facts as they stand, no matter how homely, and with all his soul he detested cant of all kinds. "His truth and his honor, his love of truth, and his love of honor, overflow all boundaries," says Mr. Birrell, "he has made the world better by his presence." [26] From this point of view the praise was fully deserved.

Yet it is just here that we come upon the weakness. And if Mark made the world better, he also made it worse; at any rate, many individuals in it. For, with the wholesale destruction of shams, went, as so often, the destruction of reverence, "that angel of the world," as Shakespeare calls it. When Mark had fairly got through with the shams, the trouble was that there was nothing left. One of his enthusiastic admirers compares him to Voltaire. The comparison is interesting and suggestive. Voltaire, too, was an enormous power in his day. He wrote for the multitude, so far as it was then possible to do it. He wielded splendid weapons of sarcasm and satire. He was always a destroyer of shams, smashed superstition and danced upon the remains of it. But Voltaire was essentially an optimist and believed in and enjoyed many things. He believed in literature, he believed in glory, above all he believed in himself. When Mark had stripped from life all the illusions that remained even to Voltaire, there was nothing left but a bare, naked, ugly, hideous corpse, amiable only in that it was a corpse, or finally would be.

Mark himself frequently recognizes this charge of being a demolisher of reverence and tries to rebut it. I never assault real reverence, he says. To pretend to revere things because others revere them, or say they do, to cherish established superstitions of art, or of morals, or of religion, is to betray and to deceive and to corrupt. But I never mock those things that I really revere myself. All other reverence is humbug. And one is driven to ask, What does he really revere himself? His instinctive reverence for humanity in individual cases is doubtless delicate and exquisite. But in theory he tears the veil from God and man alike.

To illustrate, I need only quote two deliberate and well-weighed statements of his riper years. How could you wither man more terribly than in the following? "A myriad of men are born; they labor and sweat and struggle for bread; they squabble and scold and fight; they scramble for little mean advantages over each other; age creeps upon them; infirmities follow; shames and humiliations bring down their prides and their vanities; those they love are taken from them and the joy of life is turned to aching grief. The burden of pain, care, misery, grows heavier year by year; at length ambition is dead; pride is dead; vanity is dead; longing for release is in their place. It comes at last — the only unpoisoned gift earth ever had for them — and they vanish from a world where they were of no consequence, where they have achieved nothing, where they were a mistake and a failure and a foolishness; where they have left no sign that they have existed — a world which will lament them a day and forget them forever." [27]

For those who thus envisaged man there used to be a refuge with God. Not so for Mark. Man deserves pity. God, at least any God who might have been a refuge, deserves nothing but horror and contempt. The criticism is, to be sure, put into the mouth of Satan; but Satan would have been shocked at it: he was not so far advanced as Mark: "A God who could make good children as easily as bad, yet preferred to make bad ones; who could have made every one of them happy, yet never made a single happy one . . . who mouths justice and invented hell — mouths mercy and invented hell — mouths Golden Rules, and forgiveness multiplied by seventy times seven, and invented hell; who mouths morals to other people and has none himself; who frowns upon crimes, yet commits them all; who created man without invitation, then tries to shuffle the responsibility for man's acts upon man, instead of honorably placing it where it belongs, upon himself; and finally, with altogether divine obtuseness, invites this poor, abused slave to worship him!" [28]

Can it be considered that doctrines such as this are likely to be beneficial to the average ignorant reader of democracy, or that the preacher of them made the world wholly better by his presence? It is true that they do not appear so openly in Mark's best-known books, true that the practical manliness and generosity of Tom and Huck largely eclipse them. Yet the fierce pessimism of Pudd'nhead Wilson stares at the reader from the popular story of that name and from the equally popular "Following the Equator," and even in the history of Tom and Huck the hand that slashes reverence is never far away.

The charge of evil influence fretted Mark as much as that of irreverence. He defends himself by denying that there is such a thing as personal influence from doctrines. Our happiness and unhappiness, he says, come from our temperament, not from our belief, which does not affect them in the slightest. This is, of course, an exaggeration, as the story of Mark's own life shows. I have already pointed out that in his case lack of belief did not mean lack of morals; but it does in many cases and lack of happiness in many more. One can perhaps best speak for one's self. It took years to shake off the withering blight which Mark's satire cast for me over the whole art of Europe. For years he spoiled for me some of the greatest sources of relief and joy. How many never shake off that blight at all! And again, in going back to him to write this portrait, I found the same portentous, shadowing darkness stealing over me that he had spread before. I lived for ten years with the soul of Robert E. Lee and it really made a little better man of me. Six months of Mark Twain made me a worse. I even caught his haunting exaggeration of profanity. And I am fifty-six years old and not over-susceptible to infection. What can he not do to children of sixteen?

It is precisely his irresistible personal charm that makes his influence overwhelming. You hate Voltaire, you love Mark. In later years a lady called upon him to express her enthusiasm. She wanted to kiss his hand. Imagine the humor of the situation — for Mark. But he accepted it with perfect dignity and perfect tender seriousness. "How God must love you!" said the lady. "I hope so," said Mark gently. After she had gone, he observed as gently and without a smile, "I guess she has n't heard of our strained relations." [29] Who could help being overcome by such a man and disbelieving all he disbelieved? When he clasps your hand and lays his arm over your shoulder and whispers that life is a wretched, pitiable thing, and effort useless, and hope worthless, how are you to resist him?

So my final, total impression of Mark is desolating. If his admirers rebel, declare this utterly false, and insist that the final impression is laughter, they should remember that it is they and especially Mark himself who are perpetually urging us to take him seriously. Taken seriously, he is desolating. I cannot escape the image of a person groping in the dark, with his hands blindly stretched before him, ignorant of whence he comes and whither he is going, yet with it all suddenly bursting out into peals of laughter, which, in such a situation, have the oddest and most painful effect.

Yet, whatever view you take of him, if you live with him long, he possesses you and obsesses you; for he was a big man and he had a big heart.

II
HENRY ADAMS

CHRONOLOGY

Henry Adams.
Born, Boston, Massachusetts, February 16, 1838.
Graduated at Harvard, 1858.
Private Secretary to his father in England, 1861–1868.
Assistant Professor at Harvard, 1870–1877.
Editor of the *North American Review*, 1870–1876.
Married Marion Hooper, June 27, 1872.
Wife died, December 6, 1885.
History of United States published, 1889–1891.
Education of Henry Adams privately printed, 1906.
Died, Washington, March 27, 1918.

HENRY ADAMS

II

HENRY ADAMS

I

In one of the most brilliant, subtle, and suggestive autobiographies ever written, Henry Adams informs us that he was never educated and endeavors to explain why his varied attempts at education were abortive. He flings a trumpet challenge to the universe: Here am I, Henry Adams. I defy you to educate me. You cannot do it. Apparently, by his own reiterated and triumphant declaration, the universe, after the most humiliating efforts, could not.

We should perhaps sympathize with the universe more perfectly, since Adams asks no sympathy, if, at the beginning of his narrative, or even in the middle of it, he told us what he means by education. This he never does with any completeness, though the word occurs probably as many times as there are pages in the book. When he has advanced more than halfway through his story, he remarks casually that, for a mind worth educating, the object of education "should be the teaching itself how to react with vigor and economy." [1] This is excellent, so far as it goes; but it is rather vague; it hardly seems to bear upon many of the attempted methods of education, and it does not reappear in any proportion to the demands upon it. I cannot help thinking that if in the beginning the bril-

31

liant autobiographer had set himself sincerely and soberly to reflect upon the word he was to use so often, he would have saved himself much repetition and the universe some anxiety, though he would have deprived his readers of a vast deal of entertainment. As it is, he pursues an illusory phantom through a world of interesting experiences. Probably a dozen times in the course of the book he tells us that Adams's education was ended. But a few pages later the delightful task is taken up again, until one comes to see that to have been educated, really and finally, would have been the tragedy of his life.

At any rate, nobody could furnish a prettier keynote for a portrait than the motto, "always in search of education." [2] Let us follow the search through all its meanders of intellectual and spiritual experience. From birth in Boston in 1838 to death in Washington in 1918, through America, Europe, and the rest of the world, through teaching and authorship and politics and diplomacy, through love and friendship and the widest social contact, the curious and subtle soul, with or without the afterthought of education, pursued its complicated course, scattering showers of brilliancy about it, leaving memories of affection behind it, and however difficult to grasp in its passage and elusive in its product, always and everywhere unfailingly interesting.

It is hardly necessary to say that, with this restless and unsatisfied spirit the period which sees education finished for most men did not even see it begun. The infant who starts with the definition of a teacher as "a man employed to tell lies to little boys" [3] is not very likely to get large results from early schooling. The juvenile Adams surveyed Boston and Quincy and found them distinctly wanting, in his eyes, though not in their own. "Boston had solved the universe; or had offered and realized the best solution yet tried. The problem was worked out." [4] But not for him.

With Harvard College the results were little better. He fully understood that, if social position counted, he ought to get all there was to be got. "Of money he [Adams, for the autobiography is sustained throughout in the third person] had not much, of mind not more, but he could be quite certain that, barring his own faults, his social position would never be questioned." [5] He was ready to admit also that failure, so far as there was failure, was owing precisely to faults of his own. "Harvard College was a good school, but at bottom what the boy disliked most was any school at all. He did not want to be one in a hundred — one per cent of an education." [6] Furthermore, with the willingness we all have to acknowledge weaknesses we should not wish others to find in us, he declares that "he had not wit or scope or force. Judges always ranked him beneath a rival, if he had any; and he believed the judges were right." [7] But, at any rate, Harvard did not educate him. There was no coöperation, no coördination. Everybody stood alone, if not apart. "It seemed a sign of force; yet to stand alone is quite natural when one has no passions; still easier when one has no pains." [8] And the total outcome was forlornly inadequate: "Socially or intellectually, the college was for him negative and in some ways mischievous. The most tolerant man of the world could not see good in the lower habits of the students, but the vices were less harmful than the virtues." [9]

Nobody nowadays would anticipate that Germany could do what Harvard could not. But some persons then cherished amiable delusions. Young Adams hoped vaguely that Germany might educate him. With turns of phrase that recall Mark Twain he recognizes his happy moral fitness for education — if he could get it. "He seemed well behaved, when any one was looking at him; he observed conventions, when he could not escape them; he was never quarrelsome, towards a superior; his morals were apparently good, and his moral principles, if he had any, were not known to be bad." [10]

On this admirable substructure even Germany, however, could not erect the desired edifice. Acting on the pompous encouragement of Sumner, who said to him, "I came to Berlin, unable to say a word in the language; and three months later when I went away, I talked it to my cabman," [11] he struggled with the difficulties of the German tongue and overcame them by methods of which he says that "three months passed in such fashion would teach a poodle enough to talk with a cabman." [12] But to one so exacting, the mere learning of a language was not education, though it seems so to some people. The question was, what you did with the language after you learned it. And here Germany failed as egregiously as Boston. From careful personal contact, Adams concluded that the education in the public schools was hopeless. The memory was made sodden and soggy by enormous burdens. "No other faculty than the memory seemed to be recognized. Least of all was any use made of reason, either analytic, synthetic, or dogmatic. The German government did not encourage reasoning." [13] The boys' bodies were disordered by bad air and ill-adjusted exercise, and then "they were required to prepare daily lessons that would have quickly broken down strong men of a healthy habit, and which they could learn only because their minds were morbid." [14] It was hardly likely that the university teaching would produce a more favorable impression. It did not. "The professor mumbled his comments; the students made, or seemed to make, notes; they could have learned from books or discussion in a day more than they could learn from him in a month, but they must pay his fees, follow his course, and be his scholars, if they wanted a degree. To an American the result was worthless." [15] When the time came for leaving Germany, our student departed with a light heart and a firm resolution that, "wherever else he might, in the infinities of space and time, seek for education, it should not be again in Berlin." [16]

Many earnest persons who have found direct education for themselves fruitless and unprofitable, declare that they first began to learn when they began to teach and that in the education of others they discovered the secret of their own. After a number of years of varied activity, Adams returned to Harvard as a teacher and had an opportunity to test the truth of this principle.

Viewed objectively, his work in instructing others seems universally commended. His pupils praised him, admired him, cherished a warm personal affection for him. He did not try to burden their memories, or to fill them with any theories or doctrines of his own. He made them think, he put life into them, intellectual life, spiritual life. "In what way Mr. Adams aroused my slumbering faculties, I am at a loss to say," writes Mr. Lodge; "but there can be no doubt of the fact." [17] What greater function or service can a teacher perform than this?

But for the educator himself teaching was no more profitable than learning. He had a keen sense of the responsibilities of his task. "A parent gives life, but as parent, gives no more. A murderer takes life, but his deed stops there. A teacher affects eternity; he can never tell where his influence stops." [18] He knew his own vast ignorance, as his pupils did not know theirs. "His course had led him through oceans of ignorance; he had tumbled from one ocean into another." [19] But the diffusion of ignorance, even conscientious, did not seem to him an object worth toiling for. Education, as administered at Harvard and at similar institutions, appeared to lead nowhere. The methods were wrong, the aims were wrong, if there were any aims. That it educated scholars was very doubtful; that it did not educate teachers was certain. "Thus it turned out that, of all his many educations, Adams thought that of school-teacher the thinnest." [20]

And how was it with society, with the wide and varied contact with men and women? If ever man had the chance to be educated by this means, Henry Adams was the man. He met all sorts of people in all sorts of places, met them intimately, not only at balls and dinners, but in unguarded hours around the domestic hearth. As with the teaching, others' impression of him is enthusiastic. He was not perhaps the best of "mixers" in the American sense, was shy and retiring in any general company; but he was kindly, gracious, sympathetic, full of response, full of stimulation, full of sparkling and not domineering wit. When he and Mrs. Adams kept open house in Washington, it was well said of them: "Nowhere in the United States was there then, or has there since been, such a *salon* as theirs. Sooner or later, everybody who possessed real quality crossed the threshold of 1603 H Street." [21] And again, "To his intimates — and these included women of wit and charm and distinction — the hours spent in his study or at his table were the best that Washington could give." [22]

But, as with the teaching, the man's own view of his general human relations is less satisfactory. The play of motives is interesting, certainly; but what can he learn from it, what can it do for his education? "All that Henry Adams ever saw in man was a reflection of his own ignorance." [23] The great obstacle for sensitive natures to all social pleasure, the immense intrusion of one's self, was always present to him, never entirely got rid of. "His little mistakes in etiquette or address made him writhe with torture." [24] And of one concrete, tormenting incident he says, "This might seem humorous to some, but to him the world turned ashes." [25] The annoyances were great and the compensations trifling. Though he touched many hands, heard many voices, looked deep into many eyes, he drifted through the world in a dream solitude. When he was in Cambridge, he bewailed the isolation of professors. "All these brilliant men were greedy for companionship, all were famished for want of it." [26] But the greed and the want haunted him everywhere. I do not see that they were ever satisfied.

With women he fared somewhat better than with men, and few men have been more frank about acknowledging their debt to the other sex. "In after life he made a general law of experience — no woman had ever driven him wrong; no man had ever driven him right." [27] And at all times and on all occasions he paid his debt with abundance of praise, tempered, of course, with such reserve as was to be expected from one who had all his life been seeking education and had not found it. To be sure, he readily admits entire ignorance as to the character, motives, and purposes of womankind. "The study of history is useful to the historian by teaching him his ignorance of women; and the mass of this ignorance crushes one who is familiar enough with what are called historical sources to realize how few women have ever been known." [28] But such admission of ignorance, especially for one who triumphed in ignorance on all subjects, only made it easier to recognize and celebrate the charm. One could trifle with the ignorance perpetually, elaborate it and complicate it, till it took the form of the most exquisite comprehension. "The proper study of mankind is woman and, by common agreement since the time of Adam, it is the most complex and arduous." [29]

Was it a question of the woman of America? One could write novels, like "Esther" and "Democracy," in which the woman of America is made a miracle of cleverness and is at any rate more real than anything else. Or, in intimate table-talk with great statesmen and their wives, one could calmly insist that "the American man is a failure: You are all failures. . . . Would n't we all elect Mrs. Lodge Senator against Cabot? Would the President have a ghost of a chance if Mrs. Roosevelt ran against him?" [30] But unquestionably one treads safer ground and is less exposed to the temptation of irony, if one goes back five hundred years and adores the Virgin of Chartres. With her, as Mark Twain found with Joan of Arc, one can elevate the feminine ideal to a Gothic sublimity without too inconvenient intrusion of harsh daylight.

When we reduce these abstract personal contacts to concrete individuality, we find, or divine, Adams at his best, at his most human. "Friends are born, not made, and Henry never mistook a friend." [31] For all his vast acquaintance, these friendships were not many, and they seem to have been deep and true and lasting. To be sure, he complains that politics are a dangerous dissolvent here as elsewhere. "A friend in power is a friend lost." [32] But his love for Hay and for Clarence King, not to speak of others, was evidently an immense element in his emotional life, and if they did not give him education, they did what was even more difficult and vastly better, made him forget it. Moreover, as is indicated in Mrs. La Farge's charming study of her uncle, there was a peculiar tenderness in Adams's intimate personal relations, very subtle, very elusive, very delicate, but very pervading. As is the case with many shy and self-contained natures, this tenderness showed most in his contact with the young.[33] But he had, further, a peculiar gift of eliciting by his imaginative sympathy, affectionate confidences from young and old.[34]

To what we may assume to have been the deepest love of all Adams himself makes not the faintest reference. His wooing and marriage are not once mentioned in the autobiography, but are lost in the shadowy twenty years which he passes over with a word. Some dream attachments of early childhood are touched with delicate sarcasm. Beyond this, love as a personal matter does not enter into his wide analysis. From the comments of others we infer that, although he had no children, his marriage gave him as much as any human relation can and more than most marriages do, while his wife's death brought him deep and abiding sorrow. But we may safely conclude that marriage did not give him that mysterious will-o'-the wisp, education, since, after Mrs. Adams's death, we find him seeking it as restlessly and as unprofitably as ever.

So, having traced his search through the complicated phases of the more personal side of life, let us follow it in the even more complicated development of the intelligence.

II

I⊤ would seem as if few human callings could afford a wider basis for education in the broadest sense than diplomacy, and Adams had the advantage of all that diplomacy could offer. His father cared for the interests of the Union in London all through the fierce strain of the Civil War, and Henry, as his father's secretary, saw the inside working of men's hearts and passions which that strain carried with it. He watched everything curiously, gained a fascinating insight into the peculiarities of English statesmanship, drew and left to posterity profound and delicate studies of Palmerston, Russell, Gladstone, and other figures, some not soon to be forgotten and some forgotten already. He sketched with a sure and vivid touch scenes of historic or human significance, like that of his appearance in society after the capture of Vicksburg. Monckton Milnes, who loved the North, was there; Delane, the editor of the *Times*, who did not love the North, was there. Milnes rushed at Adams and kissed him on both cheeks. Some might imagine "that such publicity embarrassed a private secretary who came from Boston and called himself shy; but that evening, for the first time in his life, he happened not to be thinking of himself. He was thinking of Delane, whose eye caught his, at the moment of Milnes's embrace. Delane probably regarded it as a piece of Milnes's foolery; he had never heard of young Adams, and never dreamed of his resentment at being ridiculed in the *Times;* he had no suspicion of the thought floating in the mind of the American minister's son, for the British mind is the slowest of all minds, as the files of the *Times* proved, and the capture of Vicksburg had not yet penetrated Delane's thick cortex of fixed ideas." [35] Saint-Simon could not have done it better.

But as to education for himself, the private secretary got nothing. In fact, these repeated, progressive, futile efforts seemed only to be carrying him beyond zero into the forlorn region of negative quantity. He found out that he was incurably shy, reserved, unfitted for the obtrusive conflicts of life. He tells us that he never had an enemy or a quarrel. But without quarrels it is difficult to win victories, even in the courteous atmosphere of diplomacy. The result of his English experience tended to little but "the total derision and despair of the lifelong effort for education." [36]

With practical politics at home in America it was the same. Only here Adams, warned by varied observation of others, made no attempt himself at even indirect personal action. It became obvious to him at a very early age that the sharp and clear decision on matters that cannot be decided, which is the first thing required of all politicians, was quite impossible for him, let alone the lightning facility in changing such decisions which gives the fine finish to a successful politician's career. He had the true conservative's dislike of innovation, not because he was satisfied with things as they are, but because he had a vast dread of things as they might be. "The risk of error in changing a long-established course seems always greater to me than the chance of correction, unless the elements

42

are known more exactly than is possible in human affairs." [37]

But if he did not seek education, where some think it is most surely to be found, in intense personal action, at least he was never tired of observing the complexities and perplexities of American political life. And if these did not give him education, they gave him amusement, as they cannot fail to do his readers in his interpretation of them. He watched the doublings and twistings and turnings of two generations of statesmen in their efforts to harmonize their own ambition with the welfare of democracy, and to him "their sufferings were a long delight," [38] while he probed their souls with the keenest and most searching analysis. His own conclusion as to the workings of American government was not enthusiastic. Cabinets were timid, congresses were helter-skelter, presidents were inefficient, even when well-intentioned, and one could not be sure that they were always well-intentioned. What wonder that the outcome of observation so dispassionate was hardly educative for the observer! It certainly is not so for his readers, except in the sense of disillusionment.

From the hard, harsh, clear-cut doings of practical America, the inquiring, acquiring spirit naturally turned at times to vaguer portions of the world, set itself to discover whether education might not come from travel and pure receptivity, since it absolutely refused to emanate from the strenuous action of common life. The results, if hardly more satisfactory, were always diverting. Rome? Oh, the charm of Rome! But it could not well be a profitable charm: "One's personal emotions in Rome . . . must be hurtful, else they could have been so intense." [39] And again, Rome was "the last place under the sun for educating the young; yet it was, by common consent, the only spot that the young — of either sex and every race — passionately, perversely, wickedly loved." [40] It might be supposed that at least travel would break up conservatism, abolish fixed habits of thought and life, supple the soul as well as the limbs, and make it more quickly receptive of innovation and experiment. Not with this soul, which found itself even more distrustful of change abroad than at home. "The tourist was the great conservative who hated novelty and adored dirt." [41]

Such a consequence might perhaps be expected from wandering in the Far East, where the flavor of dreamy repose, whether in man or nature, infected everything. But one would have thought that the bright, crystal, sparkling atmosphere of the American West might animate, enliven, induce a brisker courage and a more adventurous effort at existence. Taken beyond middle age, however, it did not induce effort, but only restlessness: "Only a certain intense cerebral restlessness survived which no longer responded to sensual stimulants; one was driven from beauty to beauty as though art were a trotting-match." [42]

And if the sunshine of the Western plains could not inspire ardor, it was not to be imagined that the gloomy silences of the Arctic Circle would produce it. They did not; they merely fed far-reaching, profound, and futile reflection on the battle of modern practical science with the old, dead, dumb, withering forces of nature. "An installation of electric lighting and telephones led tourists close up to the polar ice-cap, beyond the level of the magnetic pole; and there the newer Teufelsdröckh sat dumb with surprise, and glared at the permanent electric lights of Hammerfest." [43]

From all this vast peregrination the conclusion is "that the planet offers hardly a dozen places where an elderly man can pass a week alone without ennui, and none at all where he can pass a year." [44]

Was it better with the wanderings of the spirit than with those of the flesh? Let us see. How was it with art, the world's wide, infinitely varied, inexhaustible human product of beauty? Surely no man ever had better opportunity to absorb and assimilate all that art has power to give to any one. Yet Adams's references to the influence of art in general are vague and obscure. He can indeed multiply paradox on that, as on any subject, indefinitely. "For him, only the Greek, the Italian, or the French standards had claims to respect, and the barbarism of Shakespeare was as flagrant as to Voltaire; but his theory never affected his practice ... he read his Shakespeare as the Evangel of conservative Christian anarchy, neither very conservative nor very Christian, but stupendously anarchistic." [45] But tried by the one final, ever-repeated test, all that art offers is about as unsatisfactory as American politics or tropical dreams. "Art was a superb field for education, but at every turn he met the same old figure, like a battered and illegible signpost that ought to direct him to the next station but never did." [46]

One phase only of the vast outpouring of artistic beauty did engage the curious student, did for the time distract him wholly, involve and entangle his restless spirit in its fascinating spell, the mediæval art which he has analyzed in "Mont-Saint-Michel and Chartres." The strange glamour, the puzzling and elusive suggestion and intimation, of Gothic architecture, the complex subtleties of Christian thought and feeling, as illustrated and illuminated by that architecture, seem to have held him with an almost inexplicable charm; and the insinuating, absorbing, dominating figure of the Blessed Virgin, lit at once and shadowed by the glimmering glory of old unmatchable stained windows, gave him something, at least offered him the tantalizing image of something, that modern thought and modern wit and modern companionship could never supply.

Yet even here the final impression is that of remoteness and unreality. What can a living soul get from a dead religion? "The religion is dead as Demeter, and its art alone survives as, on the whole, the highest expression of man's thought or emotion." [47] Even to feel the art, you have to make yourself other than you are; and modern nerves, unstrung by the wide pursuit of education, cannot stand this pressure long. "Any one can feel it who will only consent to feel like a child. ... Any one willing to try could feel it like the child, reading new thought without end into the art he has studied a hundred times; but what is still more convincing, he could at will, in an instant, shatter the whole art by calling into it a single motive of his own." [48]

So we must infer that the charm of this mediæval
interlude was largely owing to its remoteness, to the
very fact that it was a world of dream and only dream,
requiring of the visitor none of the vulgar positive
action demanded by twentieth-century Washington.
And the very remoteness that made the charm took it
away; for souls of the twentieth century must live in
the twentieth century, after all.

No one lived in it more energetically than Adams, so
far as mere thinking was concerned. To turn from his
intimate acquaintance with mediæval erudition to his
equally intimate contact with the most recent movement of science is indeed astonishing. His curious
youth seized upon the theories of Darwin, twisted
them, teased them, tormented them, to make them
furnish the vanishing specific which he believed himself
to be eternally seeking. They did not satisfy him. As
time went on, he found that they did not satisfy others,
and he plunged more deeply and more widely into
others' dissatisfaction, in order to confirm his own.
The patient erudition of Germany, the logical vivacity
of France, the persistent experimenting of England, all
interested him, and from all he turned away as rich —
and as poor — as he set out. No one has more gift than
he at making scientific speculation attractive, alive, at
giving it almost objective existence, so that you seem
to be moving, not among quaint abstractions of
thought, but among necessary realities, perverse, persistent creatures that may make life worth living or
not. He embodies theory till it tramps the earth. He
treats the pterodactyl and the ichthyosaurus with the

same intimate insolence as a banker in State Street or an Adams in Quincy, and analyzes the weaknesses of terebratula with as much pride as those of his grandfather.

Yet when you reflect, you think yourself at liberty to feel a little discontent with him, since he admits so much with others. His exposition of all these scientific questions is brilliant, paradoxical, immensely entertaining. But no one makes you perceive more clearly the difference between brilliancy and lucidity. In mild, steady sunlight you can work out your way with plodding confidence; but a succession of dazzling flashes only makes darkness more intolerable. Adams can double the weight of unsolved problems upon you. He cannot — at least he rarely does — even state a problem with consistent, clear, orderly method, much less follow out the long solution of one. His most instructive effort in this line is the "Letter to Teachers of American History." Here are two hundred pages of glittering pyrotechnic. You read it, and are charmed and excited and shocked and left breathless at the end. What is the tangible result? That the investigations of modern science make it extremely doubtful whether mankind has progressed within the limits of recorded history, or ever will progress or do anything but retrograde, and that this famous discovery makes the teaching of history extremely difficult. Well, it is another added difficulty, if the discovery is correct, which Adams would be the last to affirm with positiveness. But it might have been stated in a few words, instead of being amplified and complicated with endless repetition, all the more puzzling for its brilliancy. And among the manifold serious troubles of a teacher of history, this one almost disappears from its very remoteness. Of those far more pressing, difficulties of treatment, difficulties of method, difficulties of practical interest, Adams discusses not a single one. I doubt if any teacher of history ever laid down the "Letter" with the feeling that he had been helped in any possible way.

Of the more abstract metaphysical thinking that fills the latter part of the "Education" and of "Mont-Saint-Michel," the same may be said as of the science. Its breadth is astonishing and its brilliancy incomparable. Every typical intelligence from Aristotle to Spencer is touched upon, with an especially long stop at Saint Thomas Aquinas to sum up and crystallize the whole. At first one is humbly impressed, then one is bewildered, then one becomes slightly sceptical. The result of it all seems too fluid, evanescent. Take the mysterious theory of acceleration. Through various preparatory chapters we are apparently led up to this. Suddenly we find that we have passed it, and we rub our eyes. The truth is, when analyzed, the theory of acceleration means that the nineteenth century moved rather faster than the thirteenth. But surely it needs no ghost come from the Middle Ages to tell us that. Nor does Adams's latest philosophical work, "The Rule of Phase Applied to History," improve matters much, though the idea of acceleration is further developed in it. The argument here is condensed after a fashion that would seem of itself to make lucidity difficult. But when one reflects upon such a tangle of misleading analogies, one is inclined to feel that fuller elaboration would only have left the lack of lucidity more apparent.

And we are forced to conclude, with the metaphysics, as with the science, that the thinking is more stimulating than satisfying, more brilliant than profound. There is an acute, curious, far-reaching, unfailing interest. There is not systematic, patient, logical, clarifying order and method.

Also, with the lack of method, there is another spiritual defect, perhaps even more serious. The exposition of all these high philosophical ideas is more paradoxical than passionate, and the reason is that the thinker himself had not passion, had not the intense, overpowering earnestness that alone gives metaphysical speculations value, if not for their truth, at any rate for their influence. No doubt something of the impression of dilettantism is due to the inheritance of New England reserve which Adams never entirely shook off. But the defect goes deeper, and one cannot help feeling that he approaches the profoundest questions of life and death in an attitude of amused curiosity. One must not take passages like the following too literally, and one must realize that years somewhat modified the flippancy of youth; but one must take them literally enough: "Henry Adams was the first in an infinite series to discover and admit to himself that he really did not care whether truth was, or was not, true. He did not even care that it should be proved true, unless the process were new and amusing. He was a Darwinian for fun." [49]

HENRY ADAMS

As to the last and most practical of all these varied
spiritual attempts at education, the attempt — and
the achievement — of authorship, one's conclusion is
much as with the others. The novels, the biographies,
above all, the "History of the United States," are
among the most brilliant productions of their time.
They glitter with epigrams and dazzle with paradoxes
and puzzle with new interpretations and make one
think as one has rarely thought about the problems of
American life and character. Of them all the "History"
is the most important and the most enduring. It is
fascinating in parts, almost abnormally entertaining
in parts. But even in the "History," as a whole, there is
a lack of broad, structural conception, a tendency to
obscure large movement by detail, sometimes diverting and sometimes tedious.

Moreover, I cannot help feeling the defect in Adams's
authorship that I felt in his general thinking, although
authorship was the most serious interest of his life. He
spent days in dusty muniment rooms, fortified his
pages with vast labor and consistent effort, tried his
best to make himself and others think that he was
an earnest student of history. Yet, after all his labor
and all his effort, I at least cannot escape the impression that he was an author "for fun."

III

It is precisely in this lack of seriousness that I find
the clue to the failure of Adams's whole colossal search
for education, so far as the education was anything
tangible and even the search was in any way serious.

I must repeat my ample allowance for the self-depreciation common to most autobiographies as well as for the dignified and commendable reserve with which he tells his story. Both his brother and his niece insist upon his extreme shyness and reluctance to intrude his own experiences. But, after all, reserve is rather out of place in confessions so free and intimate as those of the "Education"; and through all reserve the exposure of the inner, the inmost, life is sufficiently complete to show that the perpetual demand for education was fatal to any overpowering ecstasy. When he was a boy in college, his elders remarked that one of his compositions was notable for lack of enthusiasm. "The young man—always in search of education—asked himself whether, setting rhetoric aside, this absence of enthusiasm was a defect or a merit." [50] Whichever it was, it accompanied him always and is the main key to his vast, absorbing work. What shall be said of a man who in recounting his own life up to thirty makes no single mention of having his pulses stirred, of being hurled out of himself by nature, or love, or poetry, or God? What can any education be that is not built on some tumultuous experience of one or all of these?

Take nature. In Adams's later life there are touches that show that nature must always have had its hold on him. When he returns from Europe in 1868, he finds "the overpowering beauty and sweetness of the Maryland autumn almost unendurable for its strain on one who had toned his life down to the November grays and browns of Northern Europe." [51] Yet note even here that it is the unendurable side of passion and ecstasy that cling. And the same sense of superiority and wilful indifference peers through his wonderful rendering of still later natural experiences: "In the long summer days one found a sort of saturated green pleasure in the forests, and gray infinity of rest in the little twelfth-century churches that lined them." [52]

So with art. We have seen that he was entranced with the Middle Ages, and we have guessed that this was precisely because of their unreality to a man of the modern spirit. At any rate, there is no evidence anywhere that he was rapt or carried away by any other art whatever, either the sculpture of Greece, or the painting of the fifteenth century or of the nineteenth. "All styles are good which amuse," he says.[53] The Gothic and the Virgin amused him. When he was first overwhelmed by the sense of Beethoven's music, he describes this sense in a fashion intensely characteristic (italics mine) as "so astonished at its own existence, that he could not credit it, and watched it as something apart, accidental, and *not to be trusted*." [54] With poetry it is the same. His niece tells us he was "passionately fond of poetry." [55] I should have taken "curiously fond" to be nearer the mark. In any event, the fondness does not appear in his writings. He enlarges at huge length upon the epic and lyric productions of the Middle Ages. Except for some elaborate analyses of Petrarch — and this again is singularly characteristic — in "Esther" and "The Life of George Cabot Lodge," the poetry of the world might never have existed, for all the account his education takes of it.

I have before recognized that his utter failure to deal with the educative power of human love may be owing to a delicacy that we are bound to respect. But surely the love of God might be handled without kid gloves. Adams hardly handles it with or without them. Of course in such an extensive syllabus of non-education God has his place, with pteraspis and terebratula, and is treated with the same familiarity as those distant ancestors, and the same remoteness. Adams also insists (italics mine) that "Religion is, or *ought to be*, a feeling," [56] and in many pages of "Mont-Saint-Michel" he shows an extraordinary power of entering into that feeling by intellectual analysis. But when he seeks for the feeling in himself, the result seems to be much what he describes when he seeks it in the religious press of the world about him: "He very gravely doubted, from his aching consciousness of religious void, whether any large fraction of society cared for a future life, or even for the present one, thirty years hence. Not an act, or an expression, or an image, showed depth of faith or hope." [57] As a factor in education, God counted for little more than terebratula.

The truth is, that in this infinitely reiterated demand for education there is something too much of the egotism which Henry Adams inherited from his distinguished great-grandfather and which had not been altogether dissipated by the intermixture of two generations of differing blood, it being always recognized that egotism is perfectly compatible with shyness, reserve, and even self-effacement. In the preface to his autobiography Adams points out that the great lesson of Rousseau to the autobiographer was to beware of the Ego. In consequence Adams himself conscientiously avoids the pronoun "I" and writes of his efforts and failures in the third person. As a result it appears to me that the impression of egotism is much increased. We are all accustomed to the harmless habit of the "I"; but to have Henry Adams constantly obtruding Henry Adams produces a singular and in the end singularly exasperating effect. One cannot help asking, What does it matter to the universe if even an Adams is not educated? What does it matter if fifty years of curious experience leave him to conclude that "He seemed to know nothing — to be groping in darkness — to be falling forever in space; and the worst depth consisted in the assurance, incredible as it seemed, that no one knew more"? [58]

Not that one does not sympathize fully with the admission of ignorance. The best and the wisest, the most earnest and the most thoughtful, admit it everywhere. The vast acceleration in knowledge of which Adams complained is the distinguishing feature of the twentieth century. We are swamped, buried, atrophied in the immensity of our own learning. The specialist is the only relic of old wisdom that survives, and the specialist is but a pale and flickering torch to illuminate the general desolation.

But even here it is Adams's attitude that is unsatisfactory, not his conclusions. He proclaims that his life is spent in an effort to seek education; but one cannot escape feeling that he is not very eager to find it. He bewails the overwhelming burden of ignorance that

descends upon him, appears to bewail it; but one cannot help feeling that his grief is largely rhetorical and
that, so long as ignorance enables him to gild a phrase
or turn an epigram, he can forgive it. He "mixed himself up in the tangle of ideas until he achieved a sort
of Paradise of ignorance vastly consoling to his fa-
tigued senses." [59] "True ignorance approaches the
infinite more nearly than any amount of knowledge
can do." [60] When a student so much enjoys trifling
with the difficulties of his education, he is not likely to
make very rapid progress in overcoming them.

Simple and quiet as Adams himself was in his daily
life, the thing he most mistrusted, intellectually and
spiritually, was simplicity. "The lesson of Garibaldi,
as education, seemed to teach the extreme complexity
of extreme simplicity; but one could have learned this
from a glow-worm." [61] Again: "This seemed simple as
running water; but simplicity is the most deceitful
mistress that ever betrayed man." [62] And he disliked
simplicity because it was the key to all his difficulties,
as he himself perfectly well knew. He spent his life
tramping the world for education; but what he really
needed was to be de-educated, and this also he was
quite well aware of. He needed not to think, but to
live. But he did not want to live. It was easier to sit
back and proclaim life unworthy of Henry Adams than
it was to lean forward with the whole soul in a passionate, if inadequate, effort to make Henry Adams worthy
of life. Mary Lyon would have seemed to this wide
seeker for education very humble and very benighted;
but all Mary Lyon cared to teach her pupils was that

"they should live for God and do something." [63] If she could have communicated some such recipe to Henry Adams, she might have solved his problem, though she would have robbed the world of many incomparable phrases. And even higher — and humbler — authority than Mary Lyon declared that we must become as little children if we would enter the kingdom of heaven. Perhaps the end of the twentieth century will take this as the last word of education, after all.

III
SIDNEY LANIER

CHRONOLOGY

Sidney Lanier.
Born in Macon, Georgia, February 3, 1842.
Graduated from Oglethorpe University, 1860.
Taught at Oglethorpe University, 1860–1861.
In Confederate service during Civil War, 1861–1865.
In Union prison four months, 1864–1865.
Published *Tiger Lilies*, 1867.
Married Mary Day, December 21, 1867.
Practised law, 1868–1872.
Decided on artistic career April, 1873.
Wrote "Centennial Cantata," 1876.
Appointed lecturer on English literature, Johns Hopkins University, 1879.
Died, Lynn, North Carolina, September 7, 1881.

III

SIDNEY LANIER

LANIER lived in a spiritual whirlwind, until it snuffed him out. His whole existence was a fight with circumstances; but if every external circumstance had been easy for him, still he would have nourished a perpetual tumult and turmoil within. Our life is no dreaming idyl, but "the hottest of all battles," [1] he says himself. Again, he says of his sojourn in New York, "I am continually and increasingly amazed at the intense rate of life at which I have to live here." [2] The rate at which he always lived would have astonished some men.

Nor was the instinct of fighting wholly figurative or spiritual. As a mere child, Lanier organized a military company among his Georgia playmates, and drilled them so thoroughly that they were admitted to parade beside their elders. Before he was a man, the Civil War came, and he enlisted in the cause of his beloved South and served her with distinction. Military glory was not the kind he sought. He was not the least of a bravo or a ranter, and the references in his letters to his military experiences are few and slight. But a touch now and then shows that he knew what suffering was and what endurance was: "Did you ever lie for a whole day after being wounded, and then have water

61

brought you? If so, you will know how your words came to me." [3] And if he had felt the agony and strain of war, so he responded with the keenest thrill to its picturesqueness, its fever of excitement, its glow and glory: "Our life, during this period, was as full of romance as heart could desire. We had a flute and a guitar, good horses, a beautiful country, splendid residences inhabited by friends who loved us, and plenty of hair-breadth escapes from the roving bands of Federals who were continually visiting that Debateable Land. I look back upon that as the most delicious period of my life in many respects. Cliff and I never cease to talk of the beautiful women, the serenades, the moonlight dashes on the beach of fair Burwell's Bay . . . and the spirited brushes of our little force with the enemy." [4]

But the clash of physical war was the least part of Lanier's fierce and constant struggles with circumstance. From his youth till his death, in 1881, in his fortieth year, he had ill-health against him, had to contend not only with actual disease and pain, but with the depression and listless, hopeless discouragement, which disease and pain bring with them and leave behind them. The results of this incessant struggle were written on his face and figure, manly and dignified and noble as they were. The worn carriage showed it, the finely cut features, the deep, earnest, passionate eyes, the hands that were vigorous, but white and delicate. He understood and analyzed his condition perfectly. Sometimes he trumpeted those fits of exaltation which seem to lift the tuberculous invalid above the world:

"I feel to-day as if I had been a dry leathery carcass of a man, into whom some one had pumped strong currents of fresh blood, of abounding life, and of vigorous strength. I cannot remember when I have felt so crisp, so springy, and so gloriously unconscious of lungs." [5] But again he describes consumptives as "beyond all measure the keenest sufferers of all the stricken of this world," [6] or casually speaks of himself, "Tortured as I was this morning, with a living egg of pain away in under my collar bone." [7] Yet never for a moment could pain or lassitude subdue him or make him give up the struggle to do his work. In the splendid moments of hope he worked. In the dark, dull moments of despair he worked. He wrote "Sunrise" when his temperature was 104. He delivered his last course of lectures when so weak that his hearers feared he would expire in the chair. If ever a man died fighting, he did.

All these strains and torments of ill-health are bad enough when one has means to meet them, can afford at least the necessary lenitives, without anxiety as to where every dollar is coming from. This was far from being the case with Lanier. No one ever lived who was more indifferent to money in itself than he, who would have cared less for the excitement or the satisfaction of accumulating wealth. He did not even long for the finer luxuries and elegancies that go with wealth, though every artist can sympathize with the remark of Gray: "Swift somewhere says, that money is liberty; and I fear money is friendship too and society, and almost every external blessing. It is a great though ill-natured comfort to see most of those who have it in plenty without pleasure, without liberty, and without friends." [8] With Lanier it was a case of hard, bitter struggle for actual necessaries. Brought up in the full taste of Southern ease and abundance, he found himself, at the close of the war, like so many Southerners, beginning life in the most cramping bonds of poverty, obliged to fight his way upward from the bottom against every difficulty that material obstacles could oppose to him. Determined as he was to win success in lines of work not in themselves profitable, or only rarely and poorly so, he could not labor to get money with the single energy which is most of all necessary to achieve that result.

How desperate, how constant, how blighting this need of money was is written all through Lanier's biography and letters. Bread, mere, bare bread is the word that occurs and recurs. Indiscreet utterance "may interfere with one's already very short allowance of bread." [9] Again, "My head and my heart are both so full of poems which the dreadful struggle for bread does not give me time to put on paper." [10]

Any honest means of earning is resorted to. To all are given earnest, conscientious effort. Comfort and independence are achieved from none. Teaching? The last pitiful refuge of those who have immortal thoughts to sell? "'T is terrible work, and the labor difficulties ... make the pay very slim." [11] Government employment? It requires influence, and immortal thoughts are the last requisite for it. "I have allowed a friend to make application to every department in Washington for even the humblest position ... but without success." [12] The strain wears out body, wears out soul, wears out courage, wears out hope. "Altogether it seems as if there was n't any place for me in this world, and if it were not for May, I should certainly quit it, in mortification at being so useless." [13] To some it appears that his physical decay has a physical cause; but he finds the cause rather in "the bitterness of having to spend my time in making academic lectures and boy's books — pot-boilers all — when a thousand songs are singing in my heart that will certainly kill me if I do not utter them soon." [14]

For among all these external struggles, the most intense and passionate, made of course doubly so by the distraction of the others, was the struggle for reputation, recognition, success in the positive career, or careers, since music was almost as dear to him as poetry, that he had chosen for himself. And in this struggle, more than in any other, come the fierce alternations of hope and despair. "Through poverty, through pain, through weariness, through sickness . . . these two figures of music and of poetry have steadily kept in my heart so that I could not banish them." [15] But sometimes they hover close with intimate glory, making all life golden, and the past sacred and the future sure; sometimes they fade and shift and almost vanish, serving rather as an added torment than as a support or refuge.

In the first rapture of achievement, after the toil and travail of creation, work actually finished seems worth doing, seems never indeed a full realization of one's ideal, but seems at any rate to embody something of what one aimed at, what one hoped for. One is proud of it, if not satisfied with it, and above all one is inspired by what one has done with infinite confidence in what one can do. "So many great ideas for Art are born to me each day, I am swept away into the land of All-Delight by their strenuous sweet whirlwind." [16] And then comes the reaction and the despair. What seemed yesterday a masterpiece, to-day sounds dull and poor and tawdry, and that land of All-Delight becomes merely barren as your heart.

As some stay against this wretched self-distrust, this bankruptcy of confidence, you must have the recognition of others. There are times when your own approval is enough. There are times when it seems as nothing, and even so you cannot get it. Then a simple word of appreciation may bring heaven to you. To be sure, instead of appreciation there may be indifference and neglect, and the dread of these may tempt you to hug your own approval in self-sufficient solitude: "I'd like to send a poem or two occasionally, or an essay; but I dread rejection like a mad lover." [17] Yet you send the poem and you face the public, and if you have genius as Lanier had, the moments of recognition and glory will come, however rare, and the rarer the sweeter. To be told by an intelligent admirer "that I was not only the founder of a school of music, but the founder of American music," [18] is intoxicating, even if you do not believe it. Even more intoxicating is it to feel and see that you have carried a great company of people out of themselves, as Lanier so often did by his wonderful flute-playing. "When I allowed the last note to die, a simultaneous cry of pleasure broke forth from men and women that almost amounted to a shout, and I stood and received the congratulations that thereupon came in, so wrought up by my own playing with thoughts, that I could but smile mechanically, and make stereotyped returns to the pleasant sayings, what time my heart worked falteringly, like a mouth that is about to cry." [19]

And even such triumph is not enough for the eager spirit; but it yearns for more creation and more recognition and more and more. There is no bound, no limit, because beauty is limitless and life is limitless. To be the founder of American music would be well; but might there not be something more than that, something, who can tell what? In debating the true bent of his genius, Lanier says: "I cannot bring myself to believe that I was intended for a musician, because it seems so small a business in comparison with other things which, it seems to me, I might do." [20] And so through all the long and bitter struggle with circumstance the soul goes staggering, reaching onward, with no rest, no respite, because the outer struggle is but the image and reflection of the deeper and more passionate struggle within.

II

FOR Lanier's was none of those contented spirits who meet the battle of the world with a quiet and self-subdued mastery, who oppose to its rude shocks the unfailing tenacity of a clear and four-square purpose. With him the inner world was as full of battle as the outer. His thinking life was one long effort to solve problems, to break through difficulties instead of dodging them, to reach the last analysis of his own soul and the souls of others. "Intellectually," says one who knew him well, "he seemed to me not so much to have arrived as to be on the way, — with a beautiful fervor and eagerness about things." [21] He was always on the way, always would have been, moving, growing, developing, longing. Life could never have stood still for him, never have stagnated. There was always some problem to be met, to be fought with, to be conquered.

For such a nature the moral life meant struggle, of course. Little errors became great sins and had to be mourned over with a repentance wholly out of proportion to the fault. "My father, I have sinned. With what intensity of thought, with what deep and earnest reflection have I contemplated this lately! My heart throbs with the intensity of its anguish." [22] But the same ardor was carried into the æsthetic world, also. The enjoyment of great beauty, in music or in poetry, was not a serene enchantment, a mere ecstatic oblivion, but was sought with suffering and maintained with long effort and paid for too often with enormous lassitude. Spiritual delight is dearly bought, perhaps not too dearly bought, but dearly bought, at any rate, when it has to be described like this: "I have just concluded a half-dozen delicious hours, during which I have been devouring, with a hungry ferocity of rapture which I know not how to express, 'The Life of Robert Schumann.'" [23] And Lanier's own criticism of this same Schumann is certainly by no means true of Lanier himself: "His sympathies were not *big* enough, he did not go through the awful struggle of genius, and lash and storm and beat about until his soul was grown large enough to embrace the whole of life and the All of things." [24]

Even in matters of pure intelligence, not essentially æsthetic or emotional, even in curious metaphysical or psychological speculations, of no direct bearing on the conduct of life, Lanier showed the same intensity and activity and sincerity. To Mark Twain thought was an amusing diversion, to Henry Adams it was a splendid stimulant of curiosity, to Lanier it was a despotic master. He thought with passion, did not play with ideas or trifle with them, but threw himself upon them, fiercely determined to get rid of the rags and shroudings of tradition and convention and thrust way down to the solid structure of naked verity. "Thought, too," he says, "is carnivorous. It lives on meat. We never have an idea whose existence has not been purchased by the death of some atom of our fleshly tissue." [25] He never had, at any rate, and he paid for intellectual emancipation with throbbing fragments of his heart. He speaks somewhere of "the Latin works of Lucretius, whom I have long desired to study," [26] and in whom he found a friend. For in all literature and in all thought there is no soul who made thinking more of a battle than Lucretius did, and Lanier is like him.

It is this fighting quality of the analysis, rather than its actual result, that gives a profound interest to Lanier's critical writings. His books on the English novel and on the science of English verse may not have permanent critical value. Their ample abundance of theorizing may not always work out to a final and satisfying illumination of fact. But there is an intensity, a throb, in their spiritual movement that whirls you along with it, whether you agree or not. Indeed, the intellectual activity is too great for clarity. Every simplest element and principle is subjected to an uncompromising test of investigation and is torn to pieces with an ingenuity of insight which discovers fine threads of affinity and causality hardly perceptible to ordinary, coarser vision. Again, as with Lucretius, one feels that one is battered with a storm of solutions for problems that can be solved more simply or need not be solved at all. And, as with Lucretius, one is sometimes moved to pity, to see such a splendid intelligence wearing itself out for futile results.

But the passion for theory, for getting to the bottom of things, is infectious, just the same. It inspires Lanier's readers to-day. It inspired all who listened to his admirable lecturing at Johns Hopkins and elsewhere. The passion is manifest not only in Lanier's formal criticism, but in all his writing and thinking. "I don't mean this for a theory," he says in one case; "I hate theories." [27] But, hate them or not, he was born to theorize; not to accept blindly the theories of others, not to wallow widely in inherited formulæ: "Why do we cling so to humbugs?" [28] he cries. But into humbugs and into the crowding facts of life and into the elusive secrets of passion he loved to plunge the fine instrument of thought and twist it and turn it, with a touching confidence that it would at last lead him to the inmost shrine of truth. He was no disbeliever in intellect, no doubter of the supremacy of reason, he was not smothered with education until he came to despise it altogether, like Henry Adams. He believed that the secrets of God could be wrestled for, that every good thing was an object of combat and conquest, and that, whatever peace might be in heaven, life on this earth, to be life at all, must be perpetual war. "A soul and a sense linked together in order to fight each other more conveniently, compose a man." [29]

III

AT the same time I would not give the impression that Lanier was always fighting, that he was one of those uncomfortable persons who thrust their combative tendencies into the face of every interlocutor or house-mate. Far from it. His external battles were confined to proper occasions, and such unfailing conflict as he had within was masked by perfect control and gracious dignity and ease. To chat with him an hour you would never suspect that he carried a world war in his heart.

Moreover, like all great fighters whose fights are worth anything, he had his hours of peace, his intervals of relaxation, when he could forget the fierce violence of thought. His appeal to tranquillity does indeed seem more like a longing than a hope:

> "Oh! as thou liv'st in all this sky and sea
> That likewise lovingly do live in thee,
> So melt my soul in thee, and thine in me,
> Divine Tranquillity!" [30]

Yet even in the furious ardor of his art there were charming moments of refreshment and repose. Creation was a struggle, but the struggle of creation afforded a comparative respite from the colder and more hopeless struggle of thought. After spending long hours and long years in the endeavor to disentangle theological complications, æsthetic delight seemed at least sure and enduring, however it tantalized, and the disheartened thinker could cry, with a feeling of relief, "an unspeakable gain has come to me in simply turning a certain phrase the other way: the beauty of holiness becomes a new and wonderful saying to me when I figure it to myself in reverse as the holiness of beauty." [31]

Music, though in a sense more than any the art of struggle, though its essence seems to consist of effort for the impossible, of discords resolved only to be perpetually renewed and to seek for new resolution forever, music has its suggestions of wide quiet and all-involving peace, only the more celestial for their rarity. Writing, which at times tears the soul to shreds with its turbulent effort, which at times means only a vain, futile, exhausting wrestle with thoughts that will not be disciplined and words that flit away, writing also has its glorious compensations, when all the puzzles vanish, and sudden, splendid phrases come from unknown depths and fit into their perfect sequence with divine smooth ease. "I can't tell you with what ravishing freedom and calmness I find myself writing, in these days, nor how serene and sunny the poetic region seems to lie, in front, like broad upland fields and slopes. I write all the time, and sit down to the paper with the poems already done." [32]

And there was other more common human relaxation also, hours of putting work aside and thought aside altogether and just dabbling in sunshine and simple pleasantness. Like most Southerners, Lanier loved a good horse, and a rush through the nipping winter wind helped to shake out the creases in his soul and brush the crumbs of doubt from them. "I have at command a springy mare, with ankles like a Spanish girl's, upon whose back I go darting through the green overgrown woodpaths like a thrasher about his thicket." [33] And he found and loved the repose of Nature even more than her activity. He knew well that the best medicine for the insupportable fatigue of thought is the quiet of green fields and the mellow oblivion of autumn sunshine. Sometimes he simply touches the soothing features of the outward world and leaves the peace they brought him for the reader to divine: "The sun is shining with a hazy and absent-minded face, as if he were thinking of some quite other star than this poor earth; occasionally a little wind comes along, not warm, but unspeakably bland, bringing strange scents rather of leaves than of flowers." [34] Sometimes he makes perfectly plain what Nature does for him and what she might do for you also: "To-day you must forego expression and all outcome, you must remain a fallow field, for the sun and wind to fertilize, nor shall any corn or flowers sprout into visible green and red until to-morrow." [35]

Nor is he always serious in his relaxation, but recognizes that sweet and kindly laughter relieves tense nerves and fervid brains more completely than almost anything else, that it at once indicates that the soul is free from care and makes it so. What could be more sunny than the freakish humor that runs through the history of Bob, the mocking-bird? And laughter not only relaxed, but comforted; for the harsh pressure of circumstance, and the bitterness of neglect and rejection were made more tolerable by it. A man could not play more lightly with the peace of home after poverty-stricken wandering than in phrases like these: "I confess I *am* a little nervous about the gas-bills, which must come in, in the course of time . . . but then the dignity of being liable for such things! is a very supporting consideration. No man is a Bohemian who has to pay water-rates and a street tax. Every day when I sit down in my dining-room — *my* dining-room!— I find the wish growing stronger that each poor soul in Baltimore, whether saint or sinner, could come and dine with me. How I would carve out the merry-thoughts for the old hags! How I would stuff the big wall-eyed rascals till their rags ripped again." [36]

As these words indicate, his social, human instincts went always abreast with his love of merriment. The true life of his soul was solitary, but he would step out of it at any time to feel the warm touch of his fellows and revel in it. And his heart gave warmth as well as drank it in. His large, sunny cheerfulness was infectious, inspired cheerfulness in all about him, even strangers. As one who knew him well said, "If he took his place in a crowded horse-car, an exhilarating atmosphere seemed to be introduced by his breezy ways." [37] Or, as he himself expressed it, from the deeper, inner point of view, "any bitterness is therefore small and unworthy of a poet." [38] Not but that he had a temper, could feel a poet's fiery indignation at wrong or meanness or injustice, as when he stood up in his place, in the middle of an orchestra rehearsal, and told the conductor who had spoken brutally to a young woman at the piano just what he thought of him.[39] But the temper never hardened into sullenness, never secreted a long grudge or a blighting quarrel. "I was never able to stay angry in my life." [40]

He liked to share his pleasures with his friends, too. He recognized that music is the eminently social art and entered with a splendid, ardent zest into the common enjoyment of it. He delighted in a fascinating human mixture of tangled diversions, "Kinsfolk, men friends, women friends, books, music, wine, hunting, fishing, billiards, tenpins, chess, eating, mosquitoless sleeping, mountain scenery, and a month of idleness."[41] He stepped out with ease and grace from the exclusive society of high thoughts: "I hope those are not illegitimate moods in which one sometimes desires to surround one's self with a companionship less awful, and would rather have a friend than a god." [42] He even recognized that the friction of brains with each other is sometimes necessary to push thought to its highest: "There's not enough attrition of mind on mind here, to bring out any sparks from a man." [43]

Lastly, and perhaps in Lanier's case most important, among all the forms of refuge and repose from the harsh struggle of existence we must place the mighty solace of domestic love and home. Lanier married quite early a very charming woman, and her companionship and comfort were the greatest possible relief in all his troubles and difficulties. Though he wandered widely and his artist's calling took him among all sorts of people and made him friends with all sorts, there was nothing of the Bohemian in his nature. He loved the ties of life, all of them; did not find them ties but sweet intimacies; loved to bind the large divagation of his spirit to the quiet daily habits of hearth and home. And he shared all his ecstasies and enthusiasms with her whom he loved, so far as such things can be shared on this solitary and confining earth. If great beauty came to him in her absence, his enjoyment of it was not quite perfect, not quite satisfying without her: "For I mostly have great pain when music, or any beauty, comes past my way, and thou art not by. Perhaps this is because music takes us out of prison, and I do not like to leave prison unless thou goest also." [44] Again, "Oh, if thou couldst but be by me in this sublime glory of music! All through it I yearned for thee with heart-breaking eagerness." [45] And the solace of childhood, its grace, its gayety, its wild, wayward self-assertion, shifting into absolute dependence, varied exquisitely the mood of this higher companionship. "Nothing could be more keen, more fresh, more breezy, than the meeting together of their little immense loves with the juicy selfishness and honest animalisms of the dear young cubs." [46] While the affection for children and wife both is enlarged and interfused with the wider charity which aims to spread its all involving grasp over those near and far away and like and unlike: "Let us lead them to love everything in the world, above the world, and under the world adequately; that is the sum and substance of a perfect life." [47]

IV

YET, after all, these elements of repose and distraction, even the most sacred, were but secondary to the mighty effort and struggle to succeed, to achieve, to do great things in the world, to leave a name that should never die. And one asks one's self, as in so many similar cases, but especially with Lanier, because the struggle was so definite and so desperate, what was the motive back of it all? Why should a man fling aside health and wealth and ease and the endless variety of ephemeral diversion to give the world what it never asks for and to demand of it in return what it yields only with brutal reluctance and usually too late? What is the fierce sting, the cruel, driving spur that urges the artist onward, till one is sometimes almost tempted to conclude that genius consists in the sting itself even more than in the gifts and powers that it forces to its service?

Is it the mere desire of praise, of applause, of having men honor you and esteem you, point you out and seek your work and treasure it, *volitare per ora virorum*, as the Latin poet expressed it better than any one has expressed it since? The best and wisest have recognized this motive, sometimes frankly, sometimes reluctantly and with vain effort to hide it under other names. The young Milton knew well that

"Fame is the spur that the clear spirit doth raise."

Lanier, who analyzed and dissected everything, did not overlook the value of praise in all its forms: "Much reflection convinces me that *praise* is no ignoble stimulus, and that the artist should not despise it." [48] "Although I am far more independent of praise than formerly, and can do without it perfectly well: yet, when it comes, I keenly enjoy it." [49]

Again, besides the mere love of fame and of applause, there is in the artist the passionate desire to create things beautiful. This seems to be quite different from the appreciation of such things, though naturally such appreciation is implied in it. There are plenty of persons whose sense of all beauty is exquisite, evidently as exquisite as that of any creative artist, who yet are content to absorb and never to give out, who never apparently have the impulse to reproduce or rival the masterpieces that give them the intensest pleasure of their lives. But the artist cannot rest without the devouring effort to realize a new beauty, a different beauty, a beauty more overwhelming, more enduring than even that which intoxicates his whole being as he receives it from others. Many doubtless have felt this passion as keenly as Flaubert and Keats. None has more passionately recorded it. It is the cry that echoes in Phineas Fletcher's simple line,

"Ah, singing let me live and singing die."

It echoes everywhere in the letters of Sidney Lanier.

"It was a spiritual necessity, I must be a musician, I could not help it." [50] "The fury of creation is upon me." [51] "This unbroken march of beautiful-bodied Triumphs irresistibly invites the soul of a man to create other processions like it. I would I might lead a so magnificent file of glories into heaven." [52]

And with the instinct of creating beauty, there is the instinct of diffusing it. In some artists this appears to be lacking. They are content to achieve the beautiful, to scatter it about them, to leave it behind them, without considering or caring whether the world learns to enjoy it or not. Not theirs to create the hearing ear or the seeing eye. Let such creep in their traces and slowly arrive at comprehension. It was different with Lanier. He burned to make others feel what he felt, all that he felt. Beauty was not to be his alone, whether conceived or created. It was to light the whole wide world with a radiant glory. "We are all striving for one end," he cried, transfiguring other artists with his own ardor, and that is "to develop and ennoble the humanity of which we form a part." [53] He could not understand that musicians could be content to give subtle æsthetic emotion to a few, when it was possible to "set the hearts of fifteen hundred people afire." [54]

So we analyze vaguely, imperfectly, the deep motives that lay at the root of such a life struggle as Lanier's. Yet who shall say that we have quite touched the secret, or really, finally explained why a man should be willing to wear out his life striving, striving, striving for a goal that forever fades away?

V

As we have analyzed the nature of the struggle and its fury and its motive, so let us consider its outcome and result. There is the result for the artist himself and the result for others. And for himself there is no doubt that the struggle means life. It often means death also, as it did for Keats and for Lanier. Oftener still it means death in life, health shattered through long years, nerves broken and unstrung, quivering to utter exhaustion with misdirected effort and inadequate desire. The joy of successful creation is shot through with ardor that consumes even while it intoxicates. "Our souls would be like sails at sea; and the irresistible storm of Music would *shred* them as a wind shreds canvas, whereof the fragments writhe and lash about in the blast which furiously sports with their agony." [55] Yet withal he who has once tasted the creative rapture knows nothing else that can be called living beside it. Certainly Lanier's testimony on the point is as explicit as any one's: "To die, consumed by these heavenly fires:— that is infinitely better than to live the tepid lives and love the tepid loves that belong to the lower planes of activity." [56] And if he says so, it is beyond question true for him; for no man ever lived more fully for the rapture or died more patently from the domination of it.

And the result for others? In Lanier's case, the value of example is clear, even disregarding actual achievement. He was a Southerner, always a Southerner. He loved the South, and the South loved and loves him. And in his day the spur of that glorious spirit, ever toiling, ever hoping, giving up all material success for the long pursuit of an ideal, was the very stimulus that the young men of the South needed above all others. Who shall say that the young men of the whole country do not need and cannot profit by it now?

Moreover, Lanier's ardent struggle bore fruit in a considerable literary product. Of this the prose criticism and other writings have their value and will probably continue to be read with pleasure by a limited number. But it is the poems that give their author a permanent place in American literature. With their purely literary quality the psychographer does not concern himself. The testimony of critics of different schools is enough on this point. But to one who comes to the poems fresh from the close study of Lanier's inner life, they must necessarily prove a little disappointing. He gave them grace and dignity and charm and, above all, music; but why could he not put his soul into them? He gave them thought and observation, magic of description, and witchery of movement; but why could he not put his soul into them? Flaubert diligently kept his soul out of his novels, and the consequence is that the letters to Mademoiselle X are worth a dozen "Salammbôs" and "Education Sentimentales." But with Flaubert it was a matter of theory. With Lanier it would seem to be rather an instinctive reserve. Lucretius made all life a fight, as Lanier made it; Lucretius, of whom Lanier himself says,

"Lucretius mine
(For oh, what heart hath loved thee like to this
That's now complaining?)" [57]

Then Lucretius took the dullest subjects in the world, and, because he poured the whole of his fighting soul into them, he left the tangled thorns through which he tore his way all glorified with shreds of luminous immortality. Lanier chose the most promising, the most poetical subjects; but somehow the battling spirit is not there. As he himself most aptly says of another, "There is a certain something — a flame, a sentiment, a spark kindled by the stroke of the soul against sorrow, as of steel against flint — which he hath *not*." [58] "Sunrise" and "The Marshes of Glynn" are no doubt musical, magical, enduring poetry. But there is more to stir my spirit in the following lines, which throb with the actual passion of the long, despairing fight:

"Given, these,
On this, the coldest night in all the year,
From this, the meanest garret in the world,
In this, the greatest city in the land,
To you, the richest folk this side of death,
By one, the hungriest poet under heaven,
— Writ while his candle sputtered in the gust,
And while his last, last ember died of cold,
And while the mortal ice i' the air made free
Of all his bones and bit and shrunk his heart,
And while soft Luxury made show to strike
Her glovèd hands together and to smile
What time her weary feet unconsciously
Trode wheels that lifted Avarice to power,
— And while, moreover, — O thou God, thou God —
His worshipful sweet wife sat still, afar,
Within the village whence she sent him forth

Into the town to make his name and fame,
Waiting, all confident and proud and calm,
Till he should make for her his name and fame,
Waiting — O Christ, how keen this cuts! — large-eyed,
With Baby Charley till her husband make
For her and him a poet's name and fame." [59]

Here, at any rate, we have a shred of Lanier's heart.

IV
JAMES McNEILL WHISTLER

CHRONOLOGY

James (Abbott) McNeill Whistler.
Born, Lowell, Massachusetts, July 10, 1834.
In Russia, 1843–1848.
At West Point, 1851–1854.
Went to Paris to study, 1855.
Painted mainly in London and Paris till his death.
Ruskin trial, 1878.
Venice, 1879, 1880.
Married Beatrix (Philip) Godwin, August 11, 1888.
Wife died, May 10, 1896.
Died in London, July 17, 1903.

JAMES McNEILL WHISTLER

IV

JAMES McNEILL WHISTLER

I

THE problem with Whistler is to reconcile a great artist with a little man; or, if not a little man, an odd man, an eccentric man, a curious, furious creature, who flitted through the world, making epigrams and enemies, beloved and hated, laughing and laughable, and painting great pictures. He was glorified by his hand and damned by his tongue.

The task of disentangling this snarled soul is made much more difficult by the perplexity of records. What little he himself wrote helps, so far as it goes. But it does not go far; and we have largely to deal with a cloud of legend, sometimes rosy, sometimes lurid, according to the reporter, but always obscuring and deceitful. Anecdotes are told in a dozen different ways, and there is seldom that care for verbal authenticity which is essential with a spirit at once so precise and so evasive. The chroniclers are baffling, when they mean to be helpful. The shrewd invent, the dull misapprehend. Take a single instance. One of the best-known Whistler stories is that of the answer to a lady who declared that there was no one like Whistler and Velasquez: "Madam, why drag in Velasquez?" An obsequious follower actually inquired of the Master, whether he really meant this.[1] When they are subjected to such

Boswells, who can blame the Doctor Johnsons and the Whistlers for running riot?

Whistler was born in Lowell, like other great men. He did not like it, would have preferred his mother's Southern dwelling-place, and sometimes implied that he was born in Baltimore. He declared in court that he was born in Saint Petersburg. He once said to an inquisitive model: "My child, I never was born. I came from on high"; and the model answered, with a frivolous impertinence that charmed him, "I should say you came from below." [2] He was as reticent about his age as he was about his birthplace. But the hard fact is that he was born in Lowell in 1834. To be born in Lowell, to grow up in Russia, to be educated at West Point, to paint in France and England, with vague dashes to Venice and Valparaiso, and to die in London at seventy make a sufficiently variegated career. Even so, it was less variegated without than within.

Through the whole of it his life was in the pencil and brush, and the world to him was a world of line and color. As a small child he drew in Russia and laughed at the painting of Peter the Great. At West Point he drew his instructors, mockingly. In the Coast Survey service he made exquisite official drawings — and odd faces on the margins of them. And, till he died, laughter and fighting may have been his diversions, but drawing and painting were his serious business.

The only serious one. Few human beings have taken less interest in the general affairs of men. Even for the other arts he had little thought to spare, except as they affected his own. Poetry did not touch him, unless an occasional jingle. Tragedy he found ludicrous. He liked to fetch analogies from music, but he knew nothing about it and cared nothing for it. When Sarasate was being painted and played for him, Whistler was fascinated with the flight of the bow up and down the strings. The music escaped him.

Apparently he read little, except to gratify a special fancy. He adored Poe. He read Balzac and the writers of that group. The Pennells insist that he must have read widely, because he had so much general information. Others say that he rarely touched a book. Probably the truth is that his reading was limited, but that a most retentive memory kept forever anything that impressed him. However this may be, in all the records and biographies I have found little trace of his conversing or wishing to converse on ordinary topics of general interest.

To politics and the wide range of social questions he was utterly indifferent. He hated journalists because they talked about him and politicians because they did not. He praised America and things American at a distance, but American democracy would not have pleased him. In one sense he was democratic himself; for a street-sweeper who could draw would have interested him more than a British peer who only patronized art. "The Master was a Tory," says Mr. Menpes. "He did not quite know why; but, he said, it seemed to suggest luxury; and painters, he maintained, should be surrounded with luxury. He loved kings and queens and emperors, and had a feeling that his work should only be bought by royalty." [3]

With religion the attitude was about as elementary. Whistler dreaded death and avoided it and the thought of it.[4] He believed in a future life and could not understand those people who did not.[5] He even pushed this belief as far as spiritualism, took a lively interest in mediums and table-rappings and communications from the dead. Also, he had been brought up in a strict, almost Puritanic discipline; and the Bible had burned itself into his memory so that it colored much of his utterance. But I do not find that religious emotion or reflection had any large place in his life. He was immensely busy in this world and left the next to take care of itself. God is occasionally mentioned in his writings, but very rarely, and then with kindness, but with little interest: "God, always good, though sometimes careless." [6] In general, his religious tone is admirably conveyed by the anecdote of the dinner at which he listened in unusual silence to an animated and extensive discussion between representatives of various sects. At last Lady Burton turned to him and said, "And what are you, Mr. Whistler?" "I, madam?" he answered, using the word with which he would have liked to stop the mouths of all those who chattered about his own pursuit in life, "I, madam? Why, I am an amateur." [7]

The same ignorance of the broader thought and movement of the world very naturally permeates even Whistler's elaborate discussions of his own art. The theories of the celebrated "Ten O'Clock" lecture, that art is a casual thing, and cometh and goeth where it listeth, that the artist happens, that there are no artistic people or periods, and that art has nothing to do with history, are shrewd, apt, and, as a protest against pedantry, in many ways just. But they are incoherent and chaotic, more witty than philosophical, and more significant of Whistler than of truth. Above all, they are intimately related to the wide ignorance and indifference I have been commenting on. Whistler made much of his musical analogies. If he had thought a little more deeply on music, he might have used another — or he might not. For music is indisputably and naturally what he always sought to make painting, the art of ignorance, the art, that is, which appeals directly to the emotions and does not require for its appreciation any wide training or experience in history or the general interests of human life. It is for this reason that music, even more than painting, seems destined to become the all-engrossing, all-devouring art of the future.

And as Whistler was indifferent to human concerns outside his art in a theoretical way, so he carried the same indifference into practical action. He lived to paint, or to talk about painting; all else was pastime, and most things hardly that. Money? He could sometimes drive a hard bargain, but it was a question of pride in his own work, not of meanness. Otherwise, money slipped through his fingers, though in the early days there was little enough to slip. An artist should be comfortable, and bills were mundane things. So, while no one ever disputed his honesty of intention, he was apt to be in trouble. He was often poor and knew what privation was. But he never complained, and even when the bailiffs were in his house, he got gayety and convenience out of them as much as ever Sheridan did. With time as with money. Exact hours and art had nothing to do with each other. What was punctuality? A virtue — or vice — of the bourgeoisie. If people invited him to dinner, he came when he pleased and dinner waited. If he invited them to breakfast at twelve, they might arrive at one and still hear him splashing in his bath behind the folding-doors.[8]

In all these varied phases of simplicity and sophistication what strikes me most is a certain childlikeness. The child is a naked man, and in many respects so was Whistler. The child clue accounts for many of his oddities and reconciles many of his contradictions. He thought some strange things; but above all, he said and did what he thought, as most of us do not. Take his infinite delight in his own work. What artist in any line does not feel it? But some conceal it more than Whistler. Gazing with rapt adoration at one of his pictures, he said to Keppel: "Now, is n't it beautiful?" "It certainly is," said Keppel. And Whistler: "No, but *is n't* it beautiful?" "It is, indeed," said Keppel. And Whistler again, "raising his voice to a scream, with a not too wicked blasphemy, and bringing his hand down upon his knee with a bang so as to give superlative emphasis to the last word of his sentence," "——it! is n't it *beautiful?*"[9]

The child is the centre of his own universe, relates everything, good and evil, to himself, as does the man also in his soul. Whistler did it openly, triumphantly.

His official biographers declare that they never heard him refer to himself in the third person; but they knew him only in later life and always managed to take a comparatively academic and decorous view of him. It is impossible to question Mr. Bacher's account of his referring to himself as Whistler, though there may be some exaggeration in it. Not I, but Whistler, did this or that. You must not find fault with the work or with the word of Whistler. Or again, it was the Master, as Mr. Menpes records it for us. "You do not realize what a privilege it is to be able to hand a cheque to the Master. You should offer it on a rich old English salver and in a kingly way." [10] A good deal of mockery in it, of course, but an appalling deal of seriousness also. And note the curious coincidence of this obvious, self-asserting, third-personal egotism with the attempt of Henry Adams to avoid egotism in precisely the same manner.

Everywhere with Whistler there is the intense determination of the child to occupy the centre of the stage, no matter who is relegated to the wings. There is the sharp, vivid laugh, the screaming "Ha! Ha!" — a terror to his enemies, and something of a terror to his friends also. Not a bit of real merriment in it, but a trumpet assertion of Whistler's presence and omnipresence. There is the extraordinary preoccupation with his own physical personality. In some respects no doubt he was handsome. A good authority declares that in youth he must have been "a pocket Apollo." [11] At any rate, to use his pet word, he was always "amazing." The white lock, whether he came by it by inheritance or accident, what an ensign it was to blaze out the coming of the Master! Just so Tom Sawyer triumphed in his deleted front tooth. Read Mr. Menpes's remarkable account of Whistler at the barber's. What a sacred function, what a solemn rite, the cult of the lock, the cult of the Master's personality. At the tailor's it was the same. Every customer was called upon to give his opinion as to the fit of a coat, and the tailor was duly impressed with his almost priestly privilege: "You know, you must not let the Master appear badly clothed: it is your duty to see that I am well dressed."[12]

What wonder that Mr. Chesterton affirms, though unjustly, that "the white lock, the single eye-glass, the remarkable hat — these were much dearer to him than any nocturnes or arrangements that he ever threw off. He could throw off the nocturnes; for some mysterious reason he could not throw off the hat." [13] Milton was of the opinion that he who would be a great poet must make his own life a great poem. Whistler apparently thought that he who would be a great artist must make himself a great picture; but the picture he made was only what he detested most — the word and the thing — clever.

II

A LARGE feature of the life of children is quarreling. It certainly was a large feature of the life of Whistler. And we shall best understand his quarrels, if we think of him as a noisy, nervous, sharp-tongued, insolent boy. There have been plenty of other artists like him, alas! He has been compared to Cellini, and justly; and Vasari's accounts of Renaissance painters abound with

rough words and silly or cruel deeds that might easily
have been Whistler's. Byron's aristocratic imperti-
nences show the same thing in literature, and Heine's
noble and lovable traits were offset by abuse in the
temper of a street ragamuffin.

Whistler liked flattery and adulation as a child does,
and sought them with the candid subtlety which a child
employs for the same object, witness the singular story
of the arts and wiles with which the Master tried to
win the affection of the ignorant fishermen of Saint
Ives — without success.[14]

As he liked compliments, so he resented criticism,
especially if it did not come from a competent source;
and a competent source was too apt to mean one that
took Whistler's preëminence for granted. Criticism,
sometimes reasonable, sometimes ignorant, sometimes
really ill-natured and spiteful, was at the bottom of
most of the riotous disagreements which long made the
artist more conspicuous than his painting did. It is not
necessary to go into the details of all these unpleasant squabbles. The names of Ruskin, Wilde, Moore,
Whistler's brother-in-law, Haden, and his patrons,
Eden and Leyland, will sufficiently suggest them.
Sometimes these adventures began with hostility.
Sometimes friendship began them and hostility ended
them. Sometimes Whistler appears madly angry,
actually foaming at the mouth, says one observer, so
that a fleck of foam was to be seen on his tie.[15] Sometimes he chuckled and triumphed devilishly, with
punctuations of the fierce and irritating "Ha! Ha!"
Sometimes there was physical violence. Once the

artist caught an antagonist washing his face in a club dressing-room, slipped up behind him, dashed his head down into the soapy water, and ran away gleefully, leaving the enemy to sputter and swear.[16] Or the contest was more furious and more doubtful in outcome, as in the rough-and-tumble fights with Haden and Moore, in which each side asserted the victory. Of course such doings were disgusting and disgraceful, no matter how they resulted, and they should have been forgotten as speedily as might be.

But this was not Whistler's way. Instead, he gloated over every contest, whether verbal or muscular. He insulted his enemies and exalted their discomfiture in print, like a hero of Homer or a conceited boy. He wrote letter after letter to the papers, always so obligingly ready to help a great man expose himself. Then he collected the whole mass, including the replies of those who had been foolish enough to reply, into "The Gentle Art of Making Enemies," and flattered himself that he was a great author as well as a great painter.

Some people think he was. There is no doubt that he was a master of bitter words. His phrases have a casual ease of snapping and stinging that often scarifies and sometimes amazes. From his Puritan training and his extensive knowledge of the Bible, "that splendid mine of invective" as he characteristically called it,[17] he drew a profusion of abuse, which withered, whether justifiable or not. And occasionally he was capable of great imaginative touches that recall his pictures.

But in general his writing is vexatious and, to say the least, undignified, the angry gabble of a gifted small

boy, who ought to know better. The Wilde correspondence is perhaps the worst; but everywhere we get
a tone of cheap railing. There is a careless vigor of
sharp wit, but hardly the vituperative splendor of
Voltaire or Swift. And it is such a small, such a shallow,
such a supersensitive way of taking criticism; no ur-
banity, no serenity, no large, sweet, humorous acceptance of the inevitable chattering folly of the world.
I do not see how any admirer of Whistler's positive
genius can read "The Gentle Art" without sighing
over the pity of it.

The pity of it is rather increased by his evident enjoyment. There was no real hatred at the bottom of
his attacks. Mr. Chesterton insists that he tortured
himself in torturing his enemies. This is rather too
much of a tragic emphasis. He relieved his nervous
irritability by slashing right and left. But I do not
know that there was much torture in it and there was
a good deal of fun — of a kind. "I have been so absolutely occupied, what with working and fighting!—
and you know how I like both."[18] He did like fighting,
and winning — or to make out that he had won. In a
charming phrase he describes himself as "delicately
contentious." [19] Again, he told the Pennells that "he
could never be ill-natured, only wicked."[20] The distinction is worthy of him, and is no doubt just, though
perhaps not so self-complimentary as he thought it.

Moreover, in all his fights and quarrels, he liked and
respected — possibly, as Du Maurier insinuates,[21] —
a little dreaded — those who stood up to him and answered back. If you dodged and cowered, he would

pursue you remorselessly. If you gave him as good as he sent, he would laugh that shrill "Ha! Ha!" and let you go. Mark Twain visited him and was looking over his pictures. "Oh," cried Whistler, "don't touch that! Don't you see, it is n't dry?" "I don't mind," said Mark. "I have gloves on." From that moment they got along famously. When the artist was painting Lady Meux, he vexed and bothered and badgered her past endurance. Finally she snapped out, "See here, Jimmie Whistler! You keep a civil tongue in that head of yours, or I will have in some one to *finish* those portraits you have made of me." All Whistler could find to say was, "How *dare* you? How *dare* you?" [22]

Also, his impishness, his strange, fantastic love of mischief prompted him to scenes and touches of Aristophanic, Mephistophelian comedy, sometimes laughable and sometimes repulsive. There is a Renaissance cruelty about his remark, when told that the architect who originally designed the Peacock Room had gone mad on seeing Whistler's alterations, "To be sure, that is the effect I have upon people." [23] There is more of the ridiculous, but also much of the bitter, in his own wonderful account of his revenging himself upon Sir William Eden by spoiling the auction sale of his pictures: "I walked into the big room. The auctioneer was crying 'Going! Going! Thirty shillings! Going!' 'Ha! Ha!' I laughed — not loudly, not boisterously — it was very delicately, very neatly done. But the room was electrified. Some of the henchmen were there; they grew rigid, afraid to move, afraid to glance my way out of the corners of their eyes. 'Twenty

shillings! Going!' the auctioneer would cry. 'Ha!
Ha!' I would laugh, and things went for nothing and
the henchmen trembled." [24]

Moralizing comment on all these wild dealings and
doings of Whistler is perhaps superfluous and inappropriate. It would certainly have caused boundless
glee to Whistler himself. Yet one may be permitted to
point out how easy it is, after all, to be disagreeable and
how little real cleverness it requires. Most of us devote
our best efforts to avoiding instead of achieving it.
And then how often we fail! Even to be disagreeably
witty is not always a triumph of genius. Any tongue
can sting, and the unthinking are always ready enough
to mistake stinging for wit. Much of Whistler's recorded talk and signed writing irresistibly suggests
Doctor Johnson's saying about Cibber: " Taking from
his conversation all that he ought not to have said, he
was a poor creature."

It is the same with the gentle art of making enemies.
Most of us require no art for it, being admirably gifted
by nature in that direction. The art of making friends
is the difficult one, especially that of keeping them after
they are made. It is easy to ridicule friendship. A lady
once asked Whistler: "Why have you withered people
and stung them all your life?" He answered: "My
dear, I will tell you a secret. Early in life I made the
discovery that I was charming; and if one is delightful,
one has to thrust the world away to keep from being
bored to death." [25] And he dedicated "The Gentle
Art" to "The rare Few, who, early in Life, have rid
Themselves of the Friendship of the Many." The irony

is obvious enough, and it is equally obvious that Whistler was referring to the casual friendships of the world, which do not deserve the name. At the same time, the art, or the gift, or the instinct, of drawing men to you is worth more, to the artist or the Philistine, than that of repelling them. In studying Whistler one cannot but think of such an opposite type as Longfellow, who, without effort, almost without thought, and still keeping an individuality as sturdy and more manly than Whistler's, made himself lovable and beloved by everybody. Or, if Longfellow as an artist is not thought worthy the comparison, take Raphael, of whom Vasari tells us that a power was "accorded to him by Heaven of bringing all who approached his presence into harmony, an effect inconceivably surprising in our calling and contrary to the nature of artists." And again, "All harsh and evil dispositions became subdued at the sight of him; every base thought departing from the mind before his influence. . . . And this happened because he surpassed all in friendly courtesy as well as in art." I am inclined to think that such praise would be worth more to Whistler's memory a hundred years hence than "The Gentle Art of Making Enemies."

III

So, having got rid of the too abundant negative traits, let us turn to Whistler's attraction and charm. He was a man of contradictions, says Mr. Van Dyke; [26] and the frivolous mischief-maker lived side by side with a thoughtful, earnest, even lofty-souled artist.

The child clue will stay with us, as before. Those

who knew Whistler best frequently recur to it: "When off his guard, he was often a pathetic kid." [27] The childlike candor rarely failed, not only in asserting merits, but even in recognizing defects: "He was the most absolutely truthful man about himself that I ever met. I never knew him to hide an opinion or a thought — nor to try to excuse an action." [28] And with the candor in professing opinions went a high and energetic courage in defending them, a courage that was sometimes blatant and tactless, but seems to have been genuine, even to the point of admitting its own failures. When Mr. Menpes said to him, "Of course you don't know what fear is?" Whistler answered, "Ah, yes! I do. I should hate, for example, to be standing opposite a man who was a better shot than I, far away out in the forest in the bleak, cold early morning. Fancy I, the Master, standing out in the open as a target to be shot at!" [29]

In general human relations it would be a mistake to suppose that Whistler was always thorny, prickly, biting and stinging. His biographers insist upon his gayety.[30] Mr. Chesterton denies that he was gay at all, and I think Mr. Chesterton must have been right. True gayety not only does not wound, but cannot bear the thought of having wounded; and such was not Whistler. Though he chose the butterfly emblem, his nature had not the butterfly's light and careless saturation of sunshine. But it is true that he loved human society and did not like to be alone, even wanting people about him when he worked. He could use his wit to charm and fascinate as well as to punish. Whenever he took part in conversation, he led it and deserved to lead it. Hear this account of his appearance in a crowded club-room: "Speaking simply in a quiet way to myself, without once looking round, Whistler would draw every man in that club to his side — smart young men about town, old fogies, retired soldiers, who had been dozing in armchairs." [31] And men not only listened to him, they loved him — when they did not hate him. "Whistler could be gentle, sweet, sympathetic, almost feminine, so lovable was he." [32] He inspired deep attachments, which could be broken only by the rude knocks that he too well knew how to give them. He was gentle and patient with servants, and there is no better proof of simple goodness and kindness. [33]

For women he seems always to have had a peculiar regard, though the records of his relations with them are naturally not abundant. His Southern training and habits gave him a rather unusual formal courtesy toward them and many witnesses insist upon what is somewhat curious in consideration of his wit and comic instinct and his distinctly irregular life, that he never uttered and never tolerated grossness. Two attachments to women, at any rate, played a large part in his career. He adored his mother and obeyed her in his youth. He adored her and watched over her in his riper years. Although he resented any critical suggestion of sentiment in his portrait of her, he confided to a friend, speaking very slowly and softly. "Yes — yes — one does like to make one's mummy just as nice as possible." [34] When he was over fifty, he stumbled upon a marriage, fortuitous as most other external events in his life; but the marriage was singularly happy; he adored his wife as he had his mother, and her death shattered him in a way to confute those who denied him human tenderness.

When it comes to art, Whistler's admirable qualities are questioned by no one. His devotion to it from youth to age was perfect and unfailing. It was not perhaps so devouring and morbid a passion as with some, but it was a constant flame, which burned steadily through all difficulty and all discouragement. It was enlightened and intelligent also, directed from the beginning with firm and close discipline toward a definite object. Not that the difficulties and discouragements did not come. In spite of his confidence and belief in himself, there were times, as with all artists, when things went bitterly, hopelessly wrong: "No one," says Mr. Gay, "can realize, who has not watched Whistler paint, the agony his work gave him. I have seen him after a day's struggle with a picture, when things did not go, completely collapse, as from an illness." [35] And one should read Mr. Menpes's strange account of nervous excitement, on the very eve of an exhibition, over a mouth that was not right and could not be made right: "He became nervous and sensitive. The whole exhibition seemed to centre on that one mouth. It developed into a nightmare. At length, in despair, he dashed it out with turpentine, and fled from the gallery just as the first critic was entering." [36]

As these efforts and struggles show, no matter how much Whistler may have attitudinized in life, in art he was sincere and genuine. If you took him quietly by himself, you could not but feel this. "As a matter of fact," says Mr. Van Dyke, "he was almost always in a serious mood, and, with his knowledge and gift of language, talked most sensibly and persuasively." [37] His actions showed sincerity far more than his talk. Though he was careless about money, spent much of it and would have liked to spend more, and believed that he could have done better work if he had had more to spend, he never sacrificed one line of his ideals for any earthly payment. "It is better to live on bread and cheese and paint beautiful things than to live like Dives and paint pot-boilers," he said; [38] and he meant it and acted on it always.

Also, he was sincere enough to accept criticism and profit by it, when it came from a proper source and in a proper spirit. He once asked a great sculptor what he thought of a portrait. The sculptor, after some hesitation, merely pointed out that one leg was longer than the other. Whistler's friends expected an outburst. Instead, he remarked quietly: "You are quite right. I had not observed the fault, and I shall correct it in the morning." [39] Afterward he added, "What an eye for line a sculptor has!"

And, as he was ready to submit to intelligent criticism of his own painting, so he was equally quick to acknowledge merit in others, provided it was really there. He praised the work of students and fellow-artists with swift and discerning kindness, if it seemed to him praiseworthy. But pretence and shallow cleverness he withered wherever he found them.

JAMES McNEILL WHISTLER

His capacity for labor, for continuous and prolonged painstaking, was limitless. Because he concealed this and pretended to work lightly and casually, people thought him idle, but he was not. Industry, he said, was an absolute necessity, not a virtue, and a picture, when finished, should show no trace of the labor that had produced it: "Work alone will efface the footsteps of work." [40] In fact, it was only in age that he discovered that he had never done anything but work. "It struck me that I had never rested, that I had never done nothing, that it was the one thing I needed." [41] He could not tolerate laziness in himself or in others. In his house there were no armchairs, and to a friend who complained of this he said, "If you want to rest, you had better go to bed." [42] But his friends and pupils did not want to rest when he was with them. "Whistler invariably inspired people to work," says one who knew him well. [43] The sittings for his portraits were prolonged and repeated, till the sitters' patience was utterly exhausted, and some of them complained that the intensity of his effort seemed to draw the very life out of them. [44] In short, those who judge him by his quarrels and his bickerings and his flippancy and his odd clothes get no idea of the deep, conscientious earnestness of the artist. He worked till death to produce beautiful things. A year before he died, he insisted with passionate simplicity and sincerity: "I would have done anything for my art." [45] To the end he was looking forward and there are few finer expressions of the ardor of creation than his noble phrase, "an artist's career always begins to-morrow." [46]

IV

It is not my business to discuss Whistler's art as such. But as the general's soul is revealed in his battles and the preacher's in his sermons, so in his pictures we must seek the painter's, and the biographer must consider work as well as words.

It appears, then, that in Whistler's art there are two marked elements which, taken together, help largely to elucidate his spirit. The first of these is the element of truth, precision, exactitude, showing more conspicuously in the etchings, but never neglected in any of his work at any time. As he himself said of the Thames series of etchings: "There, you see, all is sacrificed to exactness of outline." [47]

This instinct of truth, of reality, should be closely related to the more external facts of Whistler's life. In combination with the childlike simplicity and openness, it entered largely into his everlasting quarrels. He did not quarrel in Paris — that is, not abnormally. But all the artist in him, all the truth-lover, revolted against the conventions of English Philistinism, and he fought them, whether critical or social, with all the passion that was in him. "The wit of Whistler . . . was the result of intense personal convictions as to the lines along which art and life move together," says one of his most intelligent biographers. [48] As applied to life, this instinct of truth in him was mainly destructive, and did little good to him or others; but it was obscurely lofty in aim and it was an integral part of his better nature.

JAMES McNEILL WHISTLER

In art, on the other hand, the destructive instinct led at once to construction. Here, too, indeed, there was the perpetual, deadly war on sham. Whistler saw all around him, in painting as in poetry, the Victorian excess of sentiment. The "heart interest" was what counted and execution was a minor matter. The Angelus and "Evangeline" would make a world-wide reputation, whether the workmanship was supreme or not. Against this heresy of the subject Whistler was in perpetual revolt. He did not sufficiently realize that a great artist may treat a great subject, though it too often happens that to the vulgar eye a great subject may transfigure a mean conception and a vulgar handling. He wanted to shake art free from all these adjuncts of theme and historical association and historical development and concentrate the artist's whole effort on the pure ecstasy of line and color. He pushed this so far as to revel in mere decorative richness, feeding and filling his eye and imagination with the azure and golden splendors of the Peacock Room.

But, of course, if you had pushed him home, he would have admitted that in the end all beauty must be related to human emotion, vague suggestions and intimations of subtle feeling, all the more overpowering because indefinite. And the real purpose of getting rid of a distinct, trite subject was to allow these essential emotions richer play. Music, in which he so often sought analogy, would have given it to him in this point also. For the most elaborate orchestral symphony depends as fundamentally on human emotion for its significance as does the simplest air. And

Bach and Wagner open realms of feeling equally deep, though widely different. The most original and suggestive part of Whistler's painting, if not the greatest, is that which enters most into this vast and uncharted region of intangible emotion. Of all things he loved to paint night, and what in the wide world is more throbbing with imaginative depths? "Subject, sentiment, meaning were for him in the night itself — the night in its loveliness and mystery." [49]

Here we seize the second cardinal element in Whistler's work, the element of mystery. What characterizes his range of vague emotion is not passion, not melancholy, but just the sense of mystery, of the indefinable, the impalpable. It is singular how all the critics, whatever their point of view, unite in distinguishing this, something vague, something elusive, some hidden, subtle suggestion which cannot be analyzed or seized in words. It is naturally more marked in the nocturnes and similar paintings, but it is perfectly appreciable also in the portraits and in the etchings, the handling of backgrounds and accessories, the delicate, evasive gradation of tints and shades. As Huysmans puts it, "these phantom portraits, which seem to shrink away, to sink into the wall, with their enigmatic eyes." [50]

And note that the two elements must work together to produce their full effect. It is the intense impression of definiteness, of clearness, the extraordinary realistic emphasis on one salient point, that doubles the surrounding suggestion of mystery. In the secret of making precision, vivid definition, enhance and re-

double the obscure, Whistler shows his debt to Poe
in an overwhelming degree. But there is another influence that may have affected Whistler in this regard, and that is Russia. I cannot find that any critic
or biographer has suggested this. Yet the artist passed
the most impressionable part of his youth in Russia.
His eyes, his ears, his heart were wide open all that time.
Not only Russian painting, but Russian music and
Russian feeling must have passed into them. He must
have touched the Orient there as he did later through
Japan. And surely the essence of Russian art is in
just this union of intense, bald realism with the most
subtle, far-reaching suggestion of the unlimited, the
unexplored, the forever unknown. Russia is childhood
intensely sophisticated. And so was Whistler.

It is curious to reflect that the combination in Whistler of the most lucid, direct, energetic intelligence with
the complete general ignorance I have noted earlier
led to exactly this result, of the vivid blending of precision with mystery. Clear-sighted and observant as he
was, there is no sense of modern life in him, no portrayal
of the quick, active, current movement of the contemporary world, no such portrayal of any world. The intelligence seems to clarify simply for the purpose of obscuring. The total result of the age-long development
of such a magnificent instrument as human reason,
as Whistler illustrates it, is to stultify itself, to show
with blinding flashes the boundless region of impenetrable shadow. And in this phase of Whistler's art
nothing is more symbolical and suggestive than the
nocturnes with fireworks. The glare of the falling

rocket makes the involving darkness oppress you with a negative visibility that is maddening.

It is in view of this union of intense intellectual clearness with mystery that we must read all Whistler's perplexing remarks about nature. Nature was crude multiplicity. To the unseeing eye, to the unaided imagination she would not yield her secret or tell her story. It was the artist's business and his triumph to select, to isolate, to emphasize, to coördinate, so as to suggest the emotion he wished to convey, no other and no more. Here, again, the parallel of music would have illustrated better than any analysis of painting. Every sound that music uses is given in nature, but given in a vast and tangled disorder which, to a sensitive ear, results as often in pain as in pleasure. The musician's genius brings this chaos into an ordered scheme of harmonized delight. To Whistler's artistic instinct the final and perfect triumph of human intelligence was the transforming of confusion into mystery.

Many have been puzzled by Whistler's dislike of the country and even abuse of it. The explanation is simple. In the first place, he had never lived in the country. His experience of it was the tourist's, and nature to the tourist is a mere panoramic display, a succession of vulgar excitements from an ever higher mountain or deeper sea. Nature to the tourist is scenery, not feeling. This is what Whistler meant when he returned from a visit to the English lakes and said that the mountains "were all little round hills with little round trees out of a Noah's ark"; [51] when he complained in general that there were too many trees in the country, and even grumbled to a friend, who urged the glory of the stars, "there's too many of them."[52] If he had grown up with an exquisite threshold beauty, such as hovers in the lovely lines of Cowper,

> "Scenes that soothed
> Or charmed me young, no longer young, I find
> Still soothing and of power to charm me still,"

his brush would have drawn out the charm as few had ever done before. But he dwelt in cities. Huge casual doses of nature first surfeited and then starved him. Moreover, he held, it may be justly, that the deepest fountains of mystery are not even wide fields and quiet skies, but the human eye and the human heart.

It is needless to say that the theory of mystery as I have elaborated it — perhaps too subtly — is not explicit in any writing or recorded speech of Whistler himself. When one has it in mind, however, there is a curious interest in catching the notes and echoes of it in his own words. Thus, in practical matters, take his remark to one who commented on the unfinished condition of Whistler's dwelling. "You see, I do not care for settling down anywhere. Where there is no more space for improvement, or dreaming about improvement, where mystery is in perfect shape, it is *finis*—the end — death. There is no hope, nor outlook left."[53] Or take the same instinct in a more artistic connection. "They talk about the blue skies of Italy, — the skies of Italy are not blue, they are black. You do not see blue skies except in Holland and here, where you get great white clouds, and then the spaces between are blue! and in Holland there is atmosphere, and that means mystery. There is mystery here, too, and the people don't want it. What they like is when the east wind blows, when you can look across the river and count the wires in the canary bird's cage on the other side." [54] Finally, take the wonderful words about painting in the twilight, full of mystery and vague suggestion as a poem of Shelley: "As the light fades and the shadows deepen, all the petty and exacting details vanish; everything trivial disappears, and I see things as they are, in great, strong masses; the buttons are lost, but the garment remains; the garment is lost, but the sitter remains; the sitter is lost, but the shadow remains. And that, night cannot efface from the painter's imagination." [55] Even allowing for the touch of Whistler's natural irony, such a view of art seems to amend Gautier's celebrated phrase into "I am a man for whom the *invisible* world exists," and to give double emphasis to the lines of Keats,

"Heard melodies are sweet, but those unheard
Are sweeter."

So we find in Whistler, as we found implicit in Mark Twain and Sidney Lanier and explicit in Henry Adams, the immense and overwhelming heritage of ignorance which the nineteenth century transmitted to the twentieth. But whereas Mark erected ignorance into a dogmatic religion of negation, and Adams trifled with it, and Lanier battled with it, Whistler drew out of it the enduring solace of artistic effort, and applied to its persistent torment the immortal, divine recipe for cure of headache, heartache, soul-ills, body-ills, poverty, ignominy, contempt, neglect, and pain, the creation, or even the attempted creation, of things beautiful.

V
JAMES GILLESPIE BLAINE

CHRONOLOGY

James Gillespie Blaine.

Born, West Brownsville, Pennsylvania,
    January 31, 1830.

Married Harriet Stanwood, June 30, 1850.

Removed to Maine, 1854.

Speaker of Maine House of Representatives,
    1861, 1862.

Elected to Congress, 1862.

Speaker of the House of Representatives,
    1869–1875.

Mulligan Investigation, 1876.

Senator, 1876–1881.

Secretary of State, 1881.

Nominated for the Presidency, 1884.

Secretary of State, 1889–1892.

Died, January 27, 1893.

JAMES G. BLAINE

V

JAMES GILLESPIE BLAINE

I

THE best way to get acquainted with Blaine is through
Mrs. Blaine's delightful letters. In the most natural,
most intimate fashion she reflects the whole course of
her distinguished husband's career, by glimpses and,
as it were, afar off, yet with a vividness of suggestion
and comprehension that no formal biography can equal.
And she was a most interesting person herself, a soul
of intense emotion and sympathy, of keen insight, of
playful humor, which sometimes, to be sure, developed
into a pungency of phrase not wholly beneficial to the
mistress of it. She had no love of notoriety, of great
station, oh, no! Yet what she does not want, stings
her, if she misses it; and she writes of Mrs. Cleveland,
"Feminine Frances is spelt with an 'e.' Think of the
first lady in the land, who is not your chère mère." [1]
She does not pretend to influence her husband, oh, no!
Yet the husband declares that "the advice of a sensible woman in matters of statecraft is invaluable," [2]
and what charming significance there is in the wife's
quiet remark, "He loves the confessional and the lay
sister (me) — why I do not know, as I always shrive
him out of hand." [3]

Without making any odious comparisons as to the
male objects, I must say that Mrs. Blaine's letters

115

have enabled me to understand Lady Macbeth better than ever before. There is the same mixture of adoration and fathomless pity, of warm motherly domestic comfort and eager stimulus, with which Lady Macbeth surveyed, sustained, and prompted her husband's lofty, if somewhat checkered, career. To be sure, it is difficult to imagine that Lady Macbeth could have achieved the following comprehensive eulogy; yet who can tell? "Those who know him most, love him best. I dare to say that he is the best man I have ever known. Do not misunderstand me, I do not say that he is the best man that ever lived, but that of all the men whom I have thoroughly known, he is the best." [4] Is not that a text for meditation through a long summer's day?

It may be fairly said that Blaine's whole life was political. Even in his Pennsylvania boyhood whiffs of political passion played around him, and his child letters of the forties show more interest in politics than in any other earthly thing. For a short time he taught in a blind asylum, and the wicked insinuate that he here became an adept in making the blind see whatever he wished them to. He married at twenty years of age, in 1850. He then went to Maine, to edit a paper, and for the next forty years he and politics were united so that only death could part them.

Before losing ourselves in the political vortex, however, it will be well to establish thoroughly the general elements of the man's character on which his public career was built.

His distinguishing intellectual trait was intense activity. He was a fairly wide and always an acute and comprehensive reader. He is said to have read Scott's "Napoleon" before he was eight and all Plutarch before he was nine. If so, it indicates his natural predilections. He had a singular power of abstraction in all mental labor. He did not require solitude or quiet, but could read and write and think with the whole domestic hurly-burly going on about him, and liked it. He touched all sorts of subjects lightly and vividly, with illumination, if not penetration. Mrs. Blaine goes with him to an astronomical observatory, and when they get home, comments: Mr. Blaine "demonstrates astronomically that Mars could not have any moons, and with such a scientific aroma that it would deceive the very elect, if they did not know that he does not know, and knows we know that he does not know anything about it." [5] This suggests, what is everywhere evident, that, though by no means deficient in thoughts, Blaine was on all occasions and in all connections an ingenious and unfailing master of words. It would be libelous to say that words were the whole of him. They were not, ever. But they played a large part in his life, much larger than he himself realized, and most of his writing suggests a splendid facility and felicity in words. His letters snap and sparkle with them. His "Eulogy" on Garfield, which Senator Hoar rather wildly calls, "one of the treasures of our literature," is at any rate an interesting specimen of abundant diction as well as of genuine feeling. The two bulky volumes of "Twenty Years in Congress" are almost oppressive in a verbal extension which tends to obscure their real shrewdness, common sense, and sanity.

In the same way it is somewhat difficult to get through the covering of words to Blaine's real feeling about the most serious things. When he writes to his son that "there is no success in this life that is not founded on virtue and purity, and a religious consecration of all we have to God," [6] I would not for a moment imply that he did not mean it; but it did sound well. The utter absence in Mrs. Blaine's printed letters of all religious suggestion, both for him and for her, is very noticeable; but with it we must instantly place Blaine's own fine reference to "those topics of personal religion, concerning which noble natures have an unconquerable reserve." [7] It is certain that he was zealous in his church membership, taught in Sunday-School so as to produce a lasting impression, [8] and liked at all times to discuss theology, as to discuss anything else. But he was intensely occupied with the affairs of this world and his daily attitude was quite the reverse of that of the old Scotchman whose caustic words he enjoyed putting into the mouth of a theological disputant: "I meddle only with the things o' God which I cannot change, rather than with the things o' man where I might do harm." [9]

If practical preoccupations somewhat interfered with Blaine's religion, they cut him off almost entirely from the delight of art and beauty. No doubt he talked about these things, but he had not time to feel them. When he was first in Europe, he wrote with enthusiasm of a Rubens picture and Mrs. Blaine mentions his interest in picture-buying. Yet during their long stay in Florence in the eighties it is remarkable that her letters, which speak of everything, make no reference whatever to the charm of old painting and sculpture, and in Florence too! Poetry he quoted, but neither read nor cared for. One form of art alone really took hold of him. He liked to build houses for himself and his friends and to set the houses in surroundings of exquisite natural beauty. Without having time to think much of the attractions of the external world, it is evident that he felt them.

For, if he did not care for art, the cause was lack of leisure, not lack of feeling; and his sensibility in all directions was quick and wide, perhaps profound. Mrs. Blaine's account of his emotion when writing the Garfield "Eulogy" is pathetic in the candor of its sympathy. After depleting two handkerchiefs, his only resource was to retire to solitude.[10]   Or again, the sensibility would manifest itself in keen excitement, in turbid restlessness, in the eager desire to go somewhere, see somebody, do something. The external man, as revealed to the public and to superficial observers, of course veiled all this swift impulse under decorous control. But Mrs. Blaine saw everything and tells everything, if you know how to listen to her.

Health? Blaine in his later years became morbid about his health, and at all times, though he was naturally active and vigorous, a threatening, even fancied, symptom was enough to distract him from the most important preoccupations. Even his children rallied him on the subject. "I am sorry Dr. Barker is coming on," writes Emmons, "for I can already see father furtively putting new prescriptions in his pocket and preparing himself for another conflict with modern drugs. Don't let them be alone together for a moment." [11] And Mrs. Blaine is delightful in her remorseless tenderness. Nobody could care more lovingly for real, or even for imagined ills, than she, but she understands their nature and their significance, and sets it off with delicate humor. "Your father," she says, "who always rises to the occasion of an imaginary peril, wisely skipping the real ones." [12] Is it a question of a house? "There is a house there, which he thinks would build up his health—argument with him irresistible." [13] Is it a question of an agent? "A very swell-looking young man, with dyspepsia powders, which he says are the daily food of Aldrich, Hiscock, and other great men. I see a generous box of them lying on the table." [14] And for all her love and for all her sympathy, there are moments when even her patience wavers a little. "Himself is surely improving, and were he other than the child of genius would probably not know there was anything the matter with him." [15] Again: "And with these prodigious powers, the chimney corner and speculation on his own physical condition are all that he allows himself. . . . This is one of the days when I am not in sympathy with disease." [16]

With such extreme sensibility and such proneness to imagine good and ill fortune of all kinds, it was to be expected that Blaine would be a man of the most mercurial disposition, liable to be unduly depressed or exalted. It is fascinating to watch the reflection of this tendency in the unconscious intimate record of his best beloved. Who better than she could indicate "an abasement of soul and an abandonment of hope, such as those only know who have been fed and nurtured on political aspirations and convictions"? [17] Again, she could suggest with a quiet touch the intense reaction, the eager burst of living, that was thrown into the most trivial pursuit when mounting spirits put all care and doubt behind them: "Two days of coupé, shopping (and — shall I say it without danger of being misunderstood? — your Father), reconcile me to home and a new departure."[18] While the immediate contrast has rarely been better drawn than in her vivid account of two morning greetings: " 'O Mother, Mother Blaine, I have so much to do, I know not which way to turn.' 'Good!' said I. 'Yes,' said he, 'isn't it perfectly splendid?' A very different cry from the 'O Mother, Mother Blaine, tell me what is the matter with me!' which has so often assailed my earliest waking ear, and which always makes my very soul die within me." [19]

Among the various real and fancied grounds of depression, nothing, unless considerations of his own health, affected Blaine more than considerations of his wife's. When she is ill, even not seriously, he cancels all his political engagements, and remains at her bedside, perturbed to excess, and causing more discomfort than he relieves. "In my room he sat on my bed or creaked across the floor from corner to corner by the hour, making me feel a guilty wretch to cause him so much misery. He is a dear, dear old fellow." [20]

For his family was dear to him as he was to them, and no picture of him could be complete which did not show his charm and infinite affection in the delightful atmosphere of home. His children he always speaks of with thoughtful tenderness and he not only watched over them but enjoyed them. Not many busy fathers, however loving, could have made and meant the apt reply, when asked "How *can* you write with these children here?" "It is because they *are* here that I can write." [21] And he could do more than attend to his deepest concerns in their presence. He could and did do what is perhaps even more difficult, take them into his counsels and discuss large matters of thought and profound questions of state with intimate freedom at his own fireside, thus making it, his biographer says, "the happiest fireside in the world." [22]

As for Mrs. Blaine, his tenderness for her is written all over his life and hers. It is not to be supposed that such high-mettled natures could pass long years together entirely without friction. And the husband occasionally indulges in the chaffing criticism which rather expresses tenderness than dulls it. "I drove the pair, my wife rode; she is not generally driven, but in family arrangements she more commonly drives." [23] Or directly to her, after describing a swift rush of occupations and preoccupations: "Now, was n't this making the most of a day? Had it been you, you would have sat down and cried." [24] But the depth and permanence of the tenderness are everywhere felt, even when not uttered, and they are manifested by the constant need and constant appeal far more than could be done by any power of language. The most exquisite witness to them is their reflection in Mrs. Blaine's own letters. "So much of life and so much love," she says of her family, "do not often go together." [25] And I do not know where to find summed up in briefer, more expressive words the typical attitude of a devoted wife toward an affectionate husband than in the following phrase: "I miss his unvarying attention, and as constant neglect." [26]

When it came to enlarging regard beyond the family circle, Blaine, like most busy men with happy homes, does not appear to have had any very intimate friends, at least in later life. But the list of those who were deeply attached to him is long and his unswerving loyalty to all of them is unquestioned. As to his general social qualities, it is evident that he was born to mix with men, to please them, and to succeed with them. He liked his fellows; did not like to be alone, but more than that, really liked to be with others, and there is an important difference between the two instincts. Yet, though he enjoyed society and sought it and liked to play a prominent part in it, he was always simple and natural, always himself. Mrs. Blaine catches this inimitably, as usual: "Your Father, with that independence of criticism which makes him so delightful and surprising a comrade." [27] He even carried artless candor to the point of abstraction, was careless about his appearance, careless about his clothes, would sit in a merry company entirely lost and absorbed in thought. Then he would return to himself, insist that he had not been absent, and with incomparable spirit and vivacity make up for any absence by a presence that, though never obtrusive, was all-pervading and triumphant.

When we sum up this social attraction in Senator Hoar's reference to "the marvelous personal charm of his delightful and gracious manners," [28] we are prepared to understand something of Blaine's prominent place in the political life of his time.

II

FOR, whatever else he was, and no matter what his achievement in other lines, he was always, by common consent, a consummate politician. He could sway great masses of men by his personality as few leaders in American history have been able to do. "Mr. Blaine was certainly the most fascinating man I have ever known in politics," says Andrew D. White. "No wonder that so many Republicans in all parts of the country seemed ready to give their lives to elect him." [29] To be sure, he had enemies as well as friends, and both were ardent. "There has probably never been a man in our history upon whom so few people looked with indifference," says Senator Hoar. "He was born to be loved or hated. Nobody occupied a middle ground as to him." [30] Yet even his enemies felt it difficult to resist his charm. On one occasion, when his name was mentioned at a great Democratic meeting, the whole audience rose in applause. [31] After he had made some rather irritating decision as Speaker, one Democrat was heard to say privately to another, "Now there's Blaine — but, damn him, I do love him." [32] In his later

124

years, when he was campaigning for others rather than for himself, he was everywhere received with what John Hay called "a fury of affection." [33]

Something in his appearance must have charmed people. As we look at his portraits to-day, it is not quite easy to say what this was. Indeed, in some of them there is a look about the eyes that repels. But there must have been in his manner and bearing a spirit, a vivacity, an instant response to all minds and tempers that does not get into the portraits.

At any rate, the charm was there, and was irresistible; and one searches curiously to find out the causes of it. It was effective with individuals, taken singly. And here it seems to lie largely in a subtle and instant understanding. Blaine loved to probe men's characters. He was immensely attentive to what others were saying and thinking and doing. "Your Father, whose quick ear catches everything that is said," observes his most loving critic. [34] He not only caught what was said, but he interpreted it, put two and two and ten and ten together, and built men's minds out of their common, careless actions. And as he understood, so he sympathized, showed others that he thought and also felt as they did. One of his old pupils said of his early days of teaching that when boys came to confess to him, he knew what they had to say before they spoke. [35] It was always so. He came among the people and stepped right into their lives. "Wherever man earns his daily bread by the sweat of his brow, there Mr. Blaine enters, and is ever welcome," said one of his neighbors. [36] There was some policy in this

125

undoubtedly; but there was also some love. It is impossible to dispute the admirable verdict of his biographer, "He had a passion for human happiness." [37] And it was a real passion, not a whim or fancy: life and his political pursuits were to him always a serious matter. He had plenty of jesting at his command, plenty of easy gayety. But he was never disposed to take ambition or success or the achievement of great public objects after the fashion of Seward, as an exciting game, or a neatly fashioned and highly finished work of art. He moved the souls of others because their souls and their welfare and their hopes moved him.

Also, he not only understood and felt, but he remembered, and it is impossible to overestimate the value of this gift in dealing with men. He would meet a man whom he had not seen for twenty years and recall little details of their last interview. He would shake hands with the old farmers and remember their white horses and the clever trades they made. "How in the world did he know I had a sister Mary, who married a Jones?" said one fellow, and went and voted for him.[38] He professed that the memory was instinctive, and when asked, "How can you remember so?" answered, "How can you help it?" [39] But he knew well enough that there was effort and attention in it; and attention, as Chesterfield said, is the foundation of courtesy. One day a carriage drove up. "I suspect that carriage is coming for you," said a friend. "Yes," said Blaine, "but that is not the point. The point is that there is a man on that front seat whom I have not seen for twenty-seven years, and I have got just two minutes and a half to remember his name in." [40] He remembered it.

Probably all these things together make what we call magnetism. It is interesting to hear Blaine's own opinion of this quality, as embodied in some one else. "What precisely is meant by magnetism it might be difficult to define, but it is undoubtedly true that Mr. Burlingame possessed a great reserve of that subtile, forceful, overwhelming power which the word *magnetism* is used to signify." [41] Few men have possessed more of it than Blaine.

As it attracted individuals, so it appealed to vast masses, who never came into direct contact with him at all. He was not a great orator. But he never said too much and what he did say, told. He was wonderfully quick at retort, rarely let a critic or questioner get the best of him. He was energetic and straightforward. His reputation in politics leads you to expect rhetoric in his speeches. But it is not there, or rarely. Instead, there is quick and telling common sense. And he was simple, spontaneous, appeared to speak and did speak direct from the heart, often with immediate and profound emotion. For it is characteristic of the man, and accounts for much of his success, that he combined impulse and passion with a singular degree of far-reaching foresight and control.

It was this divination and foresight, even more than his gift of speech, that enabled him to hold and guide the masses. He was a natural leader; not merely in the organizing sense, for he often left organizing to others;

but, as Senator Hoar says, he touched the people because he was like the people. [42] He saw and foresaw the issues that would animate and the right moment for introducing them; and he knew how to give them the form that clutched men's hearts.

No man has ever understood better the value as well as the defects of the American party system. His friends and his enemies were usually those of his party. He may perhaps have been inclined to favor and reward the former unduly, and it cannot be denied that he sometimes fell into extremes of partisan and personal bitterness of the sort that drove his wife to exclaim, "I hate to hate, but I am in danger of that feeling now." [43] But for the most part his grudges were laid aside as readily as they were adopted and he viewed political machinery merely as a superb agency to accomplish a particular end.

His standing as a politician, then, no one can dispute. Moreover, it is universally admitted that he was a remarkably quick, effective, and, on the whole, fair presiding officer, in the legislature and in Congress. Was he a great statesman? On one side of statesmanship, that of slow, careful, matured, solid construction, he seems to have accomplished little. His name is widely identified with a protective tariff and he spoke and worked for it all his life; but he was not connected with any actual tariff measure, unless the reciprocity element in the McKinley Bill. As secretary of state in 1881 and again, under Harrison, from 1889 to 1892, he dealt with various large questions of diplomacy. His action was always clear, incisive, and vigorous. His logic was usually reasonable and his aims patriotic. But one of his most judicious advocates speaks of his "failure in tact as a diplomatist" and admits that he was a little too prone to carry the methods of congressional debate into the sedater sphere of diplomacy. [44] And General Sherman, a connection and warm friend, says, referring to his executive ability, "His qualities are literary, not administrative. ... I would not choose Blaine to command a regiment or frigate in battle. Many an inferior man would do this better than he." [45]

On the other hand, in what may be called the imaginative side of statesmanship, Blaine was admirable. His mind lived in and with large ideas. He looked forward, far forward, as Seward did, and built ample, confident projects in the days to come. His discussions of difficult questions were almost always sane, simple, reasonable. Take, for instance, his speech on the Irish problem, at Portland, in 1886. The subject was as thorny then as it is to-day, and I do not know who has handled it with more discretion, moderation, and true wisdom than Blaine did. An even larger and more important matter was the question of Pan-America. Blaine's conception of this was far in advance of his own time, and his treatment of it, both in planning the Peace Congress and afterwards in guiding it, was enlightened and enlightening. I do not know what can be added to Mr. Root's admirable remark that Blaine had "that imagination which enlarges the historian's understanding of the past into the statesman's comprehension of the future." [46]

On the whole, most persons not blinded by party prejudice will to-day, I think, agree with Senator Hoar that Blaine would have made a satisfactory president, unless as they take exception to his financial career.

III

FROM his youth Blaine had a natural taste for business and the world of money. None of his biographers elucidates very thoroughly the transition from the poor teacher to the comfortably situated, if not wealthy, editor who at an early age threw himself into politics. But it is evident that at all times he had an instinct for speculative investments, liked the excitement of them, and needed the money. Also, in business as in politics, his taste was rather for large conception than for the slow and methodical handling of detail. One of Mrs. Blaine's delightful sentences tells, or suggests, all we need to know on this head (italics mine): "My dearer self — and certainly he might apply the title with another significance to me — is looking up his sadly neglected stocks.... All that fine Fortunatus's purse which we once held the strings of, and in which we had only to insert the finger to pay therewith for the house, *has melted from the grasp which too carelessly held it.*" [47]

And the money melted not only from careless management, but from direct expenditure. Blaine was always ready to give, always charitable. No appeal was made to him in vain. Hear another of Mrs. Blaine's quick comments on charity and business: "Father had made up his mind this morning to give five hundred dollars to the Old Ladies' Home, and it looks like a slap in the face from Providence to find things going the wrong way in the afternoon." [48]   Naturally the outgo for personal living was not less in proportion. Mrs. Blaine managed as best she could; but to bring up six children in the expensive atmosphere of Washington cost money, and it was impossible to elude the fact or to forget it.

The pressure, the financial stringency, are everywhere evident.   Mrs. Blaine's inimitable candor pushes through all her sense of decorum. "A great family are we, so far as the circulation of money is concerned. To-night we are very nearly square with the world." [49]   Again, with as near to a reflection upon "the best man she ever knew thoroughly" as she can permit herself: "I have drawn so much money this month, how can any one who never listens to or enters into a detail, understand it?" [50]   And Blaine's own dry, vivid echo fully confirms her distresses: "I do not really know which way to turn for relief, I am so pressed and hampered. . . . Personally and pecuniarily, I am laboring under the most fearful embarrassments." [51] To which he adds elsewhere this telling figure: "If I had the money myself, I would be glad to advance it to you, but I am as dry as a contribution-box." [52]

Of course this was not a constant condition. Things looked up as well as down. But money poured out, was always needed, and, as is the inconvenient nature of money, it had to come from somewhere. During the later sixties, both before and after he was established in Congress, Blaine became involved in complicated financial transactions with a certain Wan. Fisher, Jr., with whom he had become acquainted when Fisher was connected with Blaine's brother-in-law. At Fisher's instance Blaine agreed to dispose of a large amount of first-mortgage bonds of the Little Rock and Fort Smith Railroad to his friends in Maine. The bonds normally carried with them to the purchaser a considerable amount of land-grant bonds and stock; but in this case these, together with other first-mortgage bonds, were to go — privately — to Blaine as a commission. This transaction in itself appears far from creditable, but Blaine doubtless held that he was conferring a favor and deserved to be remunerated for his time and trouble. The investment did not turn out successfully. The Little Rock bonds fell, and Blaine felt himself obliged in honor — and policy — to protect his friends. About this time a considerable number of Little Rock bonds were sold to the Atlantic and Pacific and to the Union Pacific roads at a price largely in advance of the market. It was never shown that these bonds came from Blaine and he was able to advance specific evidence to the contrary. But much suspicion attached to him and in the minds of many it was never thoroughly removed. Also, there were other dealings with Fisher, more or less unsavory.

The implication through it all, of course, was that Blaine was trading on his great office as speaker of the House of Representatives and his opportunity to favor the railroads. No corrupt act was ever directly and clearly proved against him. But various passages in his letters to Fisher seemed to make the charge plausible. Shortly before taking the Little Rock bonds, Blaine had made a ruling in the House, of importance to the road. In a letter, written some time later, he points out that, while doing his plain duty, he had conferred on his new associates a considerable benefit. [53] In another letter, of earlier date, he observes, "I do not feel that I shall prove a deadhead in the enterprise, if I once embark in it. I see various channels in which I know I can be useful." [54] These phrases are certainly not conclusive; but they are damaging. They are not made less so by a sentence in one of Fisher's letters to Blaine: "Owing to your political position, you were able to work off all your bonds at a very high price; and the fact is well known to others as well as myself." [55] This charge Blaine received almost cringingly and with no denial whatever.

From the time when the unpleasant matter was first stirred up, not long before the presidential nomination of 1876, Blaine's course about it was thoroughly unsatisfactory. He made well-sounding speeches in the House, which convinced all those who were convinced already. But to any careful scrutiny it was evident that he shuffled and prevaricated, contradicted himself, and used every effort to conceal what in the end could not be concealed. He declared publicly that the very attempt to cover up an action condemns it; yet he urged upon Fisher the closest secrecy. "Burn this letter," or words to that effect, was a common phrase with him. [56] It was perhaps a natural one, but it fitted the Fisher letters too well. In the crisis of his difficulties he wrote to Fisher enclosing a letter which Fisher was to write to him, exonerating him from all blame. The document is more ingenious than ingenuous, and it is not pleasant to see a man in such a situation dictating about himself a sentence like the following: "When the original enterprise failed, I knew with what severity the pecuniary loss fell upon you, and with what integrity and nerve you met it." [57]

The reader will ask curiously how all these very private letters of Blaine's came into the evidence. The answer involves not the least disagreeable part of the whole affair. The congressional committee, which investigated the matter in the spring of 1876, called before it one Mulligan, who had been in the employ of Fisher. Mulligan had possession of the Blaine correspondence and proposed to produce it. This annoyed Blaine greatly. He had an interview with Mulligan and, according to the latter, entreated him to return the letters, resorting to suggestions of bribery and to threats of suicide. All this Blaine insisted was utterly false. What is indisputable is that he got the letters into his hands, with at least the implied promise to restore them, and then calmly put them in his pocket and walked off with them, urging that they were his own private property.

As a climax of the Mulligan business, Blaine read the letters in the House in the order and with the comments that suited him. He ended his speech characteristically by turning on the investigating committee and accusing them of suppressing, for partisan purposes, evidence that they knew would completely clear him. The attack was unjustified and, with Blaine's knowledge of the facts, discreditable; but for the moment it was immensely telling, and shortly after, as a consequence of the sudden illness which helped to prevent Blaine from being nominated, the immediate investigation was dropped. The infection of it, however, tainted his whole career.

What interests us far more than what Blaine actually did is his own attitude toward his own actions. We may assume with entire confidence that he did not for a moment admit to himself that he had done anything wrong. We have not only Mrs. Blaine's particular, triumphant, if perhaps somewhat prejudiced, assertion that he was the best man she ever knew thoroughly, but we have the general facts of human nature. An acute observer tells us that "One has always the support of one's conscience, even when one commits the worst infamies. In fact, that is precisely what enables us to commit them." The dullest of human spirits is inexhaustible in finding excuses for its own conduct, and Blaine, far from being the dullest, was one of the most brilliant.

Therefore I believe he was perfectly sincere when he declared upon the floor of the House, "I have never done anything in my public career for which I could be put to the faintest blush in any presence, or for which I cannot answer to my constituents, my conscience, and the great Searcher of Hearts." [58] These are tremendous phrases. Perhaps no living man could utter them with entire honesty, and they show the fatal, delusive power of words, for their master — and their victim. Yet I have no doubt Blaine meant them. Beyond question he meant the far more impressive words, spoken in privacy, with obviously genuine emotion: "When I think—when I think—that there lives in this broad land one single human being who doubts my integrity, I would rather have stayed — " [59] There he stopped, but his gesture showed his earnestness.

It is intensely curious to turn from these statements to the pamphlet issued in 1884 by the Committee of One Hundred and see the explicit analysis of what appear to be Blaine's six deliberate falsehoods. The thoughtful reader, who has a human heart himself, will manage to divine how Blaine explained each one of these. But it required a considerable amount of ingenuity.

Unquestionably he even excused to himself the complicated course of shuffling and concealment by which he endeavored to hide all his proceedings from the beginning. These were his own private concerns, he argued, long past and buried. The public had not conceivable business with them and he was perfectly justified in making every possible effort to put the public off the scent.

Yet, as we look back at the affair, this seems to have been his worst mistake. If at the very start he had come out with perfect candor, told the story of the whole transaction, even in its most unfortunate features, admitted that he had blundered and had been foolish as well as apparently culpable, he might have stormed the country. For the American people and all humanity love nothing better than a man who acknowledges his

136

faults, and this is the hardest of all lessons for a politician to learn. Blaine never learned it.

As to the business morality of what he did, it is of course difficult to pass a complete judgment on it, because we never shall know all the facts. But it must be remembered that in the late sixties speculation in railroads was a mania that affected most business men more or less. Lowell, who was by no means friendly to Blaine, wrote: "I suspect that few of our Boston men who have had to do with Western railways have been more scrupulous." [60] Further, it must especially be remembered that in all his long career after 1872 no suspicion of anything corrupt really attached to Blaine, although he was always interested in speculative investments. Moreover, the bitter partisan animosity that was aroused against him must always be taken into account. The most honest of the Mugwumps did not hesitate to exaggerate well-grounded suspicion into fantastic prejudice. Even Mr. Rhodes, sanest and most patient of judges, who in his eighth volume is, I think, somewhat too favorable to Blaine's statesmanship, speaks in volume seven of his "itching palm." [61] Now Blaine's palm never itched with greed. It was only slippery with liberality.

Blaine's fundamental error was when, as a great political officer of the government, he engaged in dubious speculation. Senator Hoar, who admires him and exonerates him from all wrong-doing, yet insists that "members of legislative bodies, especially great political leaders of large influence, ought to be careful to keep a thousand miles off from relations which may give rise to even a suspicion of wrong." [62] Blaine was squarely in the midst of such things and not any miles off at all. His biographer tells us that one of his favorite maxims was, "Nothing is so weakening as regret." [63] He regretted his dealings with Fisher, however, and spoke of them as "this most unfortunate transaction of my life, pecuniarily and otherwise." [64] He had reason to, for they cost him the presidency.

IV

AND the presidency may justly be regarded as the goal of his existence. There has been much argument about his own personal ambition. The biographers do not emphasize this element in him, but rather insist that, especially in later years, he became utterly indifferent to political advancement and so, repeatedly, expressed himself. No doubt he did so express himself. No doubt, after his defeat in 1884, he behaved with the utmost dignity in avoiding any insistent appeal for popular favor and in declining to have his name tossed about like a straw in the gusts of partisan debate. But those who stress this attitude too much forget that an imaginative man may perfectly well combine a passionate desire for a thing with a philosophical sense of its worthlessness. All through Blaine's career I catch gleams of intense ambition, like the brief reference to the Representatives' Hall in Maine: "That was the theatre of a great deal of early pride and power to the undersigned. It never covered the horizon of my hopes and ambitions, but while in it and of it I worked as though there was no other theatre of action in the

world." [65] And when I read Mrs. Blaine's admirable
sentence, written in 1881, "Your Father said to me
only yesterday, 'I am just like Jamie — when I want a
thing, I want it dreadfully.' " [66] I have no difficulty
in understanding Mr. Stanwood's picture of him, after
he had resigned his secretaryship of state in 1892,
shutting himself up in a Boston hotel, to follow
with passionate eagerness the reports of the Convention where his chance of touching the climax of his
fate was slipping away forever. [67]

For, no matter what view one takes of Blaine's con-
scious, personal ambition, it cannot be denied that
the total logic of his career bore him toward the presidency with a tremendous, long, unceasing sweep. He
rose upward and onward through the course of state
politics, through the larger world at Washington, suc-
ceeding everywhere and in everything, gaining friends
and supporters and admirers. It seemed in 1876 as
if the nomination must be his. Then the phantom of
the fatal Fisher stalked in and thrust him out. It was
the same in 1880. When 1884 came, the pressure of
his immense popularity was too great to be resisted
and the convention was forced to nominate him. The
campaign that followed was one of the fiercest, the
most exciting, the most personal in American history.
It was also one of the closest. To the end no one could
tell or foretell. The incident of the over-zealous Rev-
erend Burchard, who declared that his adored Blaine
was the deadly enemy of "Rum, Romanism, and Rebellion," may have affected only a few votes. But a
few in New York were enough, so few that some con-

tended that a dishonest count in a district here and there was sufficient to change the result. Yet, if it had not been for the defection of those who distrusted Blaine's financial character, a dozen Burchards could hardly have made a ripple on the wave of his immense majority.

Unfortunately we have little light on Blaine's inner life during the contest. Almost his last public words before the vote were, "I go to my home to-morrow, not without a strong confidence in the result of the ballot, but with a heart that shall not in the least degree be troubled by any verdict that may be returned by the American people." [68] The *shall* is fine. But how such words wither before the vivid humanity of Mrs. Blaine's description: "It is all a horror to me. I was absolutely certain of the election, as I had a right to be from Mr. Elkins's assertions. Then the fluctuations were so trying to the nerves. It is easy to bear now, but the click-click of the telegraph, the shouting through the telephone in response to its never-to-be-satisfied demand, and the unceasing murmur of men's voices, coming up through the night to my room, will never go out of my memory — while over and above all, the perspiration and chills, into which the conflicting reports constantly threw the physical part of one, body and soul alike rebelling against the restraints of nature, made an experience not to be voluntarily recalled." [69]

There is nothing to be said after that. For Blaine it was the end, though the end lasted for nearly ten years of lingering and superficially varied activity.

140

JAMES GILLESPIE BLAINE

After the bitterness of such an hour, what was there in life? You might preserve a decent outside, of courage, of dignity, of serenity, even of ardor and enthusiasm. Underneath there was nothing. You could nurse your pet symptoms of disease, you could turn an honest dollar in the stock market, you could trifle afar off and with no indecent coquetry with the presidential bauble, you could be a paltry secretary of state with much credit and some friction, you could see those you loved best dying about you, and, thank God, you could die yourself.

Such was the great moral tragedy of James Gillespie Blaine. With pretty much all the virtues, all the graces, all the gifts of genius, he will be remembered in his country's annals as the man who lost the presidency because he was suspected of financial dishonor.

VI
GROVER CLEVELAND

CHRONOLOGY

Stephen Grover Cleveland.

Born, Caldwell, New Jersey, March 18, 1837.

Clerk in grocery-store, Fayetteville, New York, 1851.

Removed to Buffalo, New York, 1854.

Admitted to the bar, May, 1859.

Elected Mayor of Buffalo, 1881.

Elected Governor of New York, 1882.

Elected President of the United States, 1884.

Married Frances Folsom, June 2, 1886.

Elected President of the United States, 1892.

Died, Princeton, New Jersey, June 24, 1908.

GROVER CLEVELAND

VI

GROVER CLEVELAND

I

WHAT a comfort it is to find a statesman who did not succeed by his tongue! No doubt many statesmen have admirable qualities that go a little deeper; but there are so few for whom the tongue does not open the way that gives the other qualities a chance! It was not the tongue with Cleveland, at any rate. What was it? Some say, or used to say, largely a curious concatenation of favorable circumstances. But this explains nothing, and a careful study of his character and life will make it appear otherwise.

The astounding rapidity of Cleveland's advance in the world does seem to favor the theory of accident. The son of a poor country minister, he had to make his way, and made it. He began to earn his living as a boy in a grocery-store, in Fayetteville, New York. Oddly enough, like his great rival, Blaine, he later held a position in a blind asylum. Afterwards he found entrance into a lawyer's office and by immense industry gradually established a solid practice. He was district attorney and sheriff of Erie County, but not exceptionally active or prominent in politics. Then, in 1881, at the age of forty-four, he became mayor of Buffalo, in 1882 governor of New York, in 1884 president of the United States, in 1892 president for a second term. Is it strange that when he was first in the White House he should have said, "Sometimes I wake at night and rub my eyes and wonder if it is not all a dream?" [1]

How far was personal ambition a driving force in this extraordinary progress? If you will listen to Cleveland's eulogists, you will think it was mainly absent. According to them it would appear that great office called for such a man as he was and he complied with the demand much against his good nature. It needs but little knowledge of the human heart to find this view somewhat exaggerated. Men may distrust their own ability. They may weary of public cares and burdens. But few men have high dignity actually thrust upon them. I have no doubt that Cleveland liked to be governor, liked to be president, especially relished all his life the grandeur of having filled those offices.

This does not mean that there was any untruth in his statement that "I never sought an office of any kind in my life." [2] It does not mean that he would have sacrificed one grain of self-respect to gain any office. As dignities came to him, he accepted and enjoyed the honor of them; but what they brought chiefly was duty. He set himself earnestly, strenuously to fulfil that duty, and the task was so absorbing that he hardly perceived the necessary result of such fulfilment in another step outward and upward. When the presidential nomination came to him in 1884, he was occupied with his gubernatorial duties at Albany. Naturally he had divined what was coming, or others had obligingly divined it for him. But neither the nomination nor the campaign distracted him for a moment from his regular work. He stayed in his office and let others do the talking, or, if they talked too loudly around him, he went off for a day's fishing and forgot them. The campaign was ugly, saturated with abuse and scandal. He paid no attention. Tell the truth, he urged, and take the consequences. He appeared so little before the campaigning crowds that the sight of a great, surging, triumphant assembly was nearly too much for him. In an almost broken voice he said: "I never before realized what was expressed in the phrase 'a sea of faces' — look at it; as beautiful and yet as terrible as the waves of the ocean." [3]

The honest earnestness of his attitude through it all shows in nothing better than in his way of receiving the news of his nomination. As he sat working in his office, firing was heard outside. "They are firing a salute, Governor, over your nomination," said General Farnsworth. "That's what it means," added Colonel Lamont. "Do you think so?" said the governor quietly. "Well," he continued, "anyhow, we'll finish up this work." [4] That was the man. Whatever happens, life or death, we'll finish up this work.

II

WITH so much work and so little talk, it was natural that the country should not have known a great deal about the man it had elected president. It never did know him. It has only begun to know him since his death. Even to-day it is difficult to penetrate beneath the apparent stolidity, the calm, unshaken, impersonal reserve, to the warm, human soul. And we have no such charming, indiscreet confidences as lurk and linger in the letters of Mrs. Blaine. But there was a human soul there, just the same.

There was intelligence, solid, substantial, reliable, if not broad. Early opportunities of education there had not been. The fierce necessities of bread and butter cut them off, and they were always deeply, perhaps excessively, regretted. There are some evidences of desultory reading, for instance a rather surprising reference to Sterne,[5] and an out-of-the-way quotation from "Troilus and Cressida." [6] But in the main large culture was not the foundation of Cleveland's thought or life.

Nor was the lack of cultivation supplemented, as so often, by quickness or alertness of intelligence. Some men appear learned, and even are learned, by seizing the end of a thread here, another there, and patching all together into a respectable fabric of wide conversance. This process was foreign to Cleveland's nature. He did not generalize, did not move readily and swiftly among abstract ideas, did not spring instantly to the far-reaching significance of the immediate. It is true, we have a most interesting saying of his, "I can never understand the meaning of any theory until I know how it happened." [7] But this implied apparently rather the lawyer's close and curious search for precedent than the scientist's ample reach into the infinite relations of things.

On the other hand, if the intelligence was not swift or restless, it was vigorous, thorough, and exact. Once a problem was fairly stated, it had to be solved, and it had to be solved rightly. I cannot make this clearer than by quoting a most discerning account of Cleveland's methods in conversation, which were evidently his methods in all intellectual activity. "At first there was a gradual approach to the question from one side, and then, perhaps after a little pause, unexpectedly from another. He was exploring, looking around, feeling his way, searching for the general dimensions. He literally 'went around' the subject carefully and cautiously, and on all sides. And if some part necessary to its completeness was lacking, he made a note of it, and took it into account all the way to the end of his discourse. When he had made his tour around the subject, as could be noticed by a penetrating word here or a phrase of discovery there, his work was almost done, and with one step he went straight to the centre of the complex question. And then he was done, and the talk was ended." [8]

A great deal has been said about Cleveland's manner of writing. It is interesting to us because it is thoroughly significant of the man and of his intellectual quality. It is formal, elaborate, almost artificially literary, and people are surprised that a nature so simple, in some respects so primitive, should adopt such conventional expression. They do not see that it is precisely because he was simple, reserved, an actor not a talker, that his effort in words was labored and far-fetched. Perfect simplicity and directness of form come naturally to those to whom words are an inborn gift. Those who deal by instinct with deeds, when they do talk, are apt to talk

AMERICAN PORTRAITS

ponderously. Yet when Cleveland put the hammer of his character behind his words, they beat themselves into the memory of the nation, and few presidents have supplied history with more phrases that are remembered.

Cleveland's general intellectual qualities are admirably illustrated in his spiritual and religious attitude. The metaphysics of religion had no attraction for him. He did not care to discuss speculative theology; and so-called higher criticism, with its fine-spun analyses and subtle interpretation of scripture, was extremely distasteful to his practical bent. He had a certain fine, large, human tolerance, well shown in his excellent story of the Old Baptist whom his Presbyterian friends tried to get into their church: "No; you folks are Presbyterians, and if I go over to your church I could n't enjoy my mind." [9] He liked to enjoy his own mind and to let others enjoy theirs. Nevertheless, his personal religion was essentially conservative. What his father had preached and his mother had practised was all he needed. "The Bible is good enough for me," he said; "just the old book under which I was brought up. I do not want notes, or criticisms, or explanations about authorship or origin, or even cross-references. I do not need or understand them, and they confuse me." [10]

It is true that, like other human beings, he did not always practise as he preached. There were irregularities in his earlier life of a sort to scandalize his mother. And his summer church attendance was not quite what his father would have approved. But if he did not always go to church, he rigidly respected

150

the Sabbath. And he had all his life a fineness of conscience rather notable in a man of such wide experience of the world and so practical a temper. When he was offered a considerable sum for a magazine article, he refused to take so much because he had accepted less for a similar contribution. [11] Again, he writes to a friend that he has declined an offer of a position "to which was attached a very large salary, because I did not think I could do all the situation demanded and make the project a success." [12] Still more striking is the account of his remorse over a possible misstatement in connection with a fishing adventure. Long after the incident occurred, he spoke of it with obvious distress and when told that with the circumstances as they were, his story must have been exact, he assented doubtfully: "I hope so, I hope so." [13]

It is evident that the æsthetic element of religion would not have had much appeal for Cleveland. And in purely æsthetic matters he was even less responsive. It is interesting and curious to think that a man who had such a vast influence and held such a prominent position should have been utterly cut off from emotional pleasures which mean the sweet of life to so many people. Of course this is not peculiar to him. Still, few even practical men are more completely indifferent to the attraction of art and beauty. Of painting, of music, he seems to have known little or nothing. He liked the old hymns and had learned many of them by heart. In the illness of his later years he read many novels. But he went to his grave, as do millions of others, less prominent, with no consciousness whatever of what great art is and does for us.

To the beauty of nature he was much more susceptible, and Mr. West has admirably preserved the account of one experience which must have been representative of hundreds. "I can't find a word for it," he said quietly . . . after a flood of sunshine had burst through a light April shower. "What makes it so beautiful? There is no word good enough. 'Ravishing' comes nearest, I think. Where does it come from? Do you know what I mean? It is too good for us. Do you understand me? It is something we don't deserve." [14]

The dumb but pervading sense of such natural beauty is bound up with what was always one of the greatest delights of Cleveland's life, outdoor sport. He was an ardent fisherman and hunter. His little book of fishing sketches brings one right close to him, brings one right inside the garment of formal, conventional reserve more than anything else possibly could. You seem to be spending days of large, quiet pleasure with him, in the woods and on the water, to be hearing his quaint stories and shrewd comments, and entering into feelings that he never showed to congressmen or reporters. The very effort and simple artifice of the expression reveal a simple nature doing its best to make refractory words convey what it seeks to utter and cannot. Under the calm, controlled surface you divine latent possibilities of excitement which could be aroused by keen sport as well as by human rivalry. There is temper there, there is depression there and discouragement, there is intense enthusiasm. There is the suggestion of imaginative range, also, though it is instantly checked by gentle irony. "The keen delights of imagination which should be the cheering concomitants of the most reputable grade of duck-hunting." [15]

It is characteristic of Cleveland's conservative temper that his passion for sport was not modified into any of the later nineteenth-century equivalents. It was simply the hearty, out-of-doors expression of full-blooded health and vigor. There is no sign of the slightest scientific curiosity connected with it. There is no pretentious humanitarianism. The object of hunting was killing; not wanton or wasteful, but plain killing, for the excitement to be extracted from it. Yet it must not for a minute be supposed that he was a hard or cruel man. He was much the contrary. Lowell's keen vision detected this on slight contact: "With all his firmness he has a very tender and sympathetic nature, or I am much mistaken." [16] The tenderness showed in many ways. Even as to animals there was an almost exaggerated sympathy, when they were not objects of sport. He once worried for days because he had not interfered to protect a cat which some boys were chasing. [17] He had all the horror of death which is natural to persons of energetic vitality. [18] He had the deepest pity for suffering and the pity tended quickly to take active forms of relief.

He had especially one of the surest signs of sensibility and tenderness, a constant love and appreciation of children. He felt their sorrows. "The cry of a child always distressed him. It made him quite miserable sometimes when he was walking through the village. He always wanted to stop and find out what was the matter." [19] Their sports and spirits amused him and he entered into them quietly but keenly, as if he were a child himself. Children understood this, as they always do. General Wood, who knew Cleveland well, says, "He was as fond of children as was Lincoln. He understood them, and they instinctively knew it and felt it, and they came to him as a friend." [20]

It is notable that this intimacy with children often goes with a rather reserved and generally unsociable temperament. We have noticed the same thing in the case of Henry Adams. It was strikingly true of General Lee as of Cleveland. The explanation is simple. Children ask sympathy and attention. They never ask you to give yourself. To Cleveland, as to Lee, the conventional restraints of formal society were irksome. Cleveland could indeed supply charming platitudes on social duty, as in the Fishing Sketches, "Every individual, as a unit in the scheme of civilized social life, owes to every man, woman, and child within such relationship an uninterrupted contribution to the fund of enlivening and pleasurable social intercourse." [21] This recalls the pretty saying of the old dramatist, "Oh, my lord, we are all born in our degrees to make one another merry." [22] But Cleveland avoided the obligation when he could, hated long dinners and pompous ceremonies, and on such occasions would often sit perfectly silent and not manifest an overpowering interest in the talkativeness of others.

He hated the display and luxury and extravagance of society, also. He believed that a nation showed its sanity in its simplicity, and the attacks in his writings on the money craze of his contemporaries and their mad rush for wealth are so frequent as almost to suggest a hobby. He practised frugality as well as preached it, cared nothing for costly clothes or fare or ornament. One day, during Cleveland's second presidential term, a train stopped at the Gray Gables station. "Look," called the conductor to the passengers, impersonally, "there's Mrs. Cleveland and Grover on the platform." The passengers looked. "Well," said one woman, "if I had fifty thousand dollars a year, I would n't dress like that." [23]

It must not be for a moment supposed, however, that Cleveland's economy arose from any taint of meanness. He was as indifferent to the accumulation of money as to the spending of it. He tells us so himself, speaking of the sacrifice of several thousand dollars for an unnecessary scruple, "But I don't deserve any credit for that, because money has never been a temptation to me." [24] And others, many others, bear him out. Even in his early law practice "he was always indifferent and careless as to his fees. His clients had to offer him money." [25] And the failure to accumulate arose not only from indifference, but from wide generosity. Without the least ostentation, he helped many a poor and struggling applicant — and non-applicant — over difficulties and tight places. When he left the law, his partner wrote: " I am now closing up a case of Cleveland's which has been running on for years, during all which time he had paid all disbursements . . . because the man was too poor to meet these necessary expenses. And this is only one case out of many that are here on our books." [26]

The assertion that Cleveland avoided general society does not mean that he did not appreciate human relations. To be sure, he found politics rather detrimental to friendship. Where there is so much to give, casual affection is apt to look for what may be got and to wither when disappointed. Also, such firm and self-centred natures are less disposed to form human ties than those which naturally turn to others for advice and comfort and support. But for that very reason the friendships formed are founded on a deeper comprehension and sympathy and are usually loyal and permanent. In the last years of his life, Cleveland wrote some touching words about his own—perhaps imagined—deficiencies in the matter of human association and about his love and longing for it. "I have left many things undone I ought to have done in the realm of friendship ... and still it is in human nature for one to hug the praise of his fellows and the affection of friends to his bosom as his earned possession." [27] Certainly no one can read Gilder's charming "Record of Friendship" without finding in it all the evidence of deep and genuine feeling. And the close intimacy of Cleveland and Joseph Jefferson, so different in character and in their life-interests, yet each so finely tempered in his own way, is one of the pleasant traditions of American biography.

Cleveland's personal affection went even deeper in his domestic relations than with his friends. His mother's memory and the depth of her tenderness were treasured all his life. When he was elected governor of New York, he wrote to his brother, "Do you know that if mother were alive, I should feel so much safer?" [28]

After McKinley's term had begun, he said: "I envy him to-day only one thing and that was the presence of his own mother at his inauguration. I would have given anything in the world if my mother could have been at my inauguration." [29] All the glimpses that we get of his own home life, with wife and children, are charming: simple, devoted, sympathetic, undemonstrative, but participant of joy and grief alike.

And in all these intimate relations with those who knew him best, the quiet, shy, reserved Cleveland of general society melted and mellowed into the best of company and the most responsive of listeners and talkers. "He had a real 'gift' of silence," says one of his biographers; [30] that is, he could be silent in a way to chill impertinence and curiosity and again, in a very different fashion, to inspire enthusiasm and tempt confidence. And then, with the right company, he would talk himself, would drop reserve and restraint and give out his hope and heart with singular and engaging frankness and so simply that you almost saw the life right through the severing veil of speech.

The picture of Cleveland in these elementary social connections would be quite incomplete without recognition of his very attractive and winning humor. People who know him only as the heavy and somewhat solemn official do not appreciate this. Yet even in public addresses he could indulge in a vein of pleasantry, as when, in comparing the legal and medical professions, he says that the defeated client has the privilege of swearing not only at the court, but at his lawyer, but "the defeated patient, on the contrary, is very quiet indeed and can only swear at his doctor if he has left his profanity in a phonograph to be ground out by his executor." [31] And the same tone creeps into the dignified veto of a pension bill: "Whatever may be said of this claimant's achievements during his short military career, it must be conceded that he accumulated a great deal of disability." [32] All the evidence goes to show that in conversation Cleveland could relish a joke and make one, less often perhaps with pointed wit than with those shrewd, quiet turns of ironic humor so dear to the American heart. The "Fishing Sketches" are permeated through and through with simple fun of just this sort, which at its best sometimes recalls the frolic fancy of Lamb, although it is a Lamb with the slightly cumbrous gambol of an elephant. "The ways of fishermen are inexplicable," says this august follower of the craft. "The best fishermen do not attempt it; they move and strive in the atmosphere of mystery and uncertainty, constantly aiming to reach results without a clue, and through the cultivation of faculties, non-existent or inoperative in the common mind." [33] And again, fishermen, "to their enjoyment and edification, are permitted by a properly adjusted mental equipment to believe what they hear." [34]

III

FROM the preceding analysis of Cleveland's personal qualities, it will be evident that in some respects he was not adapted to political success. Few great statesmen have made themselves, by their own def-

inite action in behalf of right, more deliberately unpopular. Cleveland himself was perfectly aware of this
and could even state it with a certain grim enjoyment.
In speaking of one of his vetoes as governor, he said:
"Before I was married, I used sometimes to talk to
myself when I was alone, and after the veto, that night,
when I was throwing off my clothes, I said aloud:
'By to-morrow at this time I shall be the most unpopular man in the State of New York.'"[35] He had little
or none of that tact which enables some men to ingra-
tiate themselves more in refusing than others when
they grant. Shyness, reserve, obstinate determination
to do right regardless of anybody's feelings, are all far
from being passports to triumph in American politics.

Moreover, Cleveland hated publicity and was al-
wa: s suspicious and distrustful of newspapers and
representatives of the press. He had no tincture of the
useful art of appearing to tell them everything and
telling them nothing. He had an excellent memory,
and a paper which had once criticized him unjustly,
or, even worse, ridiculed him, was disliked and avoided.
Though self-controlled and self-contained in all his
passions, journalistic indiscretion was more likely than
anything else to arouse him to a burst of temper. Of his
many snubs to reporters perhaps none was more apt
than the remark to a young fellow who was trying to
elicit comment on some question of foreign policy:
"That, sir, is a matter of too great importance to discuss
in a five-minute interview, now rapidly drawing to its
close." [36] The retort was shrewd, but not calculated to
promote affection.

On the other hand, even politicians and journalists could not fail to appreciate Cleveland's great public merits. There is his honesty, his infinite candor. Said one journalist, after an attempt to get something, "He is the greatest man I ever met — and he wouldn't promise to do a thing I wanted." [37] Nothing touches the American people like straightforward truth-telling. When Cleveland's youthful morals were impeached and he said at once, "Tell the facts," he won more votes than any possible subterfuge could have gained for him. Veracity was a habit with him, it was constitutional. It was so ingrained that, as a fisherman, he could even afford to make a jest of it and give as the principle of that fraternity, "In essentials — truthfulness; in non-essentials — reciprocal latitude." [38] When it was a matter of life, not fishing, there was no question of jest. His son once brought out the truth under great temptation to the contrary, and Cleveland remarked to a near friend that the boy "evidently was going to be like him; because untruthfulness seemed to be no temptation whatever to either of them." [39]

And as his candor appealed to the American nation, so did his democratic way of living and thinking. He knew the common people, he had passed all his early life in intimate contact with them, and watched them and studied them with insight and sympathy, saying little, but seeing much. Lowell, with his quick discernment, said of him, "He is a truly American type of the best kind — a type very dear to me, I confess." [40] He grasped the large daily facts of human nature, because his own temperament was peculiarly and singly based on them. He needed no effort to enter into common lives, because his own life was common, in the best sense. He would fish all day with an old farmer and swap long stories with him and then incidentally get and give homely views about political questions. When, as governor, he was walking down to the State House at Albany, if he came up with the blind crier of the courts, he would take his arm and help him along over the crossings, and let the business of his great office wait. [41]

He cannot be said to have won votes by pure oratory. He was not a natural speaker, had not a trace of the magnetism that carries vast multitudes away in a storm of excitement. At the same time, especially in later life, his speeches told. He prepared them with the utmost care and delivered them with dignity and measured ease, and every hearer felt that they had character and purpose behind them. Even his appearance, while never splendid or imposing, carried the stamp of the square, determined energy which conquers the world.

These things touched the general public. But how was it with the political managers? Cleveland is generally supposed to have been weak here. His admirers often urge that all his success was gained not through the politicians, but in spite of them, and that he did not stoop to or understand the ordinary methods by which the political game is played. Their arguments are to a certain extent borne out by his own remark, "This talk about the importance of 'playing politics'

— look at the men who have played it. Have they got as far, after all, as I have?" [42] On the other hand, he was not so wholly ignorant as some supposed. He knew men thoroughly, and such knowledge is the first requisite of political success. Moreover, even character will not make a man governor of New York, without some acquaintance with political machinery. And against the above comment of Cleveland we can set another, which may not contradict but certainly amplifies it: "Somehow there seems to have been an impression that I was dealing with something I did not understand; but these men little knew how thoroughly I had been trained, and how I often laughed in my sleeve at their antics." [43]

Also, in political management as in everything else, labor counts. Cleveland's superb physical strength and tireless industry enabled him to attend to details which others are forced to neglect. He always knew what was going on, and this is the first step to controlling it. He believed in doing your own work, doing it carefully and systematically, and leaving nothing to chance. There is an immense secret of achievement in the apparently two-edged compliment of Tilden as to his distinguished follower: "He is the kind of man who would rather do something badly for himself than to have somebody else do it well." [44]

And Cleveland had another element of political success. He was an intense party man. We have seen the pleasant humor which played over the surface of his temperament. But it did not enter into his politics. Life was not a game to him, as it was to Seward, or

a dainty work of art. He took the Democratic party
with an almost appalling seriousness. Over and over
he reiterates that the salvation of the country, if
not the salvation of the world, must be accomplished
by the Democrats. His elaborate statement of the
Democratic creed in 1891 is, to be sure, fairly general;[45] but its possibility of fulfilment was, for him,
completely bound up with Democratic organization.
"Of all the wonders that I have seen during my life,"
he said, "none has quite so impressed me as the reserve power of the Democratic party, which seems to
have the elements of earthly immortality."[46] And
within a few months of his death he gave cordial
assent to the most sweeping possible declaration of
party principle: "Whatever your own party may do,
it is always a mistake to vote for a Republican."[47]

Yet, from what we have already seen of the man,
it is hardly necessary to say that he never sacrificed
and never would have sacrificed duty, as he saw it,
to any party consideration. At an early stage in his
career he wrote officially: "I believe in an open and
sturdy partisanship, which secures the legitimate
advantages of party supremacy; but parties were
made for the people, and I am unwilling, knowingly,
to give my assent to measures purely partisan, which
will sacrifice or endanger their interests."[48] He never
did give his assent to such. When he was being considered as a candidate for a third nomination, he
declared, "If I am ever president of this country
again, I shall be president of the whole country, and
not of any set of men or class in it."[49]

And, however he may have disapproved of Republican principles, he was always fair and even friendly toward Republican individuals. His repeated judgment of McKinley and of McKinley's administration showed the broadest appreciation of practical difficulties and the keenest sympathy with honest effort.

Further, he did not hesitate to fight the objectionable elements in his own party, wherever he found them. "We love him for the enemies he has made," said General E. S. Bragg at the time of his first nomination. [50] The American people loved him for those enemies and do still. But the wire-pulling and ring-running politicians in the Democratic party did not love him and at times he seemed more severed from them than from even the Republicans. Colonel Watterson declares that "He split his party wide open. The ostensible cause was the money issue. But underlying this there was a deal of personal embitterment. . . . Through Mr. Cleveland the party of Jefferson, Jackson, and Tilden was converted from a Democratic into a Populist." [51] This is an exaggerated view. Yet it is certain that lack of political tact, and perhaps an increasing fixity in his own opinions, fostered by too great disregard of criticism, brought Cleveland into a vast amount of friction. Speaking of him and Harrison, Henry Adams says, in his epigrammatic fashion, "Whatever harm they might do their enemies, was as nothing when compared to the mortality they inflicted on their friends." [52] There was trouble with friends and enemies both. Cleveland's difficulties with the Senate are matter of history and, although he may have had abstract reason on his side, the results for his administrative usefulness could not but be harmful.

Also, all these public conflicts were isolating, produced a feeling of helplessness and depression, even in a temperament so calm and solid as his. In 1894 he wrote, "There never was a man in this high office so surrounded with difficulties and so perplexed and so treacherously treated and so abandoned by those whose aid he *deserves*, as the present incumbent. But there is a God, and the patriotism of the American people is not dead; nor is all truth and virtue and sincerity gone out of the Democratic party." [53] The patriotism of the American people is not dead yet, and the very isolation which at the time seemed to prove the president unpractical and impracticable, serves to-day to increase his dignity and to place him secure above all parties as a great American.

IV

BUT let us elucidate a little more definitely what Cleveland actually stands for in American history; since it must be supposed that the man whose summing up of official duty gave rise to the phrase, "Public office is a public trust," [54] and who gave his life to working from that text, must have left some memorial of permanent significance.

It may be recognized at once that this memorial is not to be sought mainly in positive, progressive achievement. Cleveland would not, of course, have denied the possibility or desirability of progress. Some of his utterances, especially as to the accumulation of wealth, have a radical tone which sounds like the advanced twentieth century. Still, it cannot be said that he initiated great movements or changes of any kind. Even his most positive efforts, as with the tariff and civil service reform, like his splendid private usefulness in the insurance world, were in the nature of a return to purer and saner ideals, an endeavor to put public business on the basis of thrift and common sense which is absolutely necessary to success in the conduct of private affairs.

For the man was essentially, by habit and temperament, a thorough conservative. It may seem a little surprising to find such a type in the Democratic party, at least in the North. To understand this, we must appreciate the wholesome, admirable truth that in our American system each of the two major parties is capable of being either conservative or radical. We usually think of the Republicans as conservative, entrenched in tradition and custom. Yet the cardinal principle of Republicanism is the strength and vitality of the federal government, and, as the most far-reaching progress and radical change must come through that government, it is natural that radical and progressive elements should be constantly found in Republican alliance. On the other hand, while the Democrats suggest radicalism, their two fundamental tenets have always been the reduction of all government interference to the lowest terms and in especial a jealous assertion of the state governments against the federal.

Under the American Constitution these two principles mean instinctive, persistent conservatism.

It is thus that we find Cleveland, in the midst of so many radical, disturbing elements, the incarnation of conservatism, of a firm, insistent, reiterated negative. The value of such a negative force in any popular government may be measured by the difficulty of maintaining it. To say no, is the ordinary politician's stumbling-block. Even when he is forced to say it, he mouths it with qualifying adjectives and explanations, seeking in vain to mix the opposing bitter with the seducing sweet. "Blaine and I," said Garfield, ". . . have too much pain in the refusals we have constantly to make." [55]

This was never the trouble with Cleveland. A good, round, sonorous no came from him without the slightest difficulty and there was no disputing and no revoking it. From this point of view even his limitations were a help to him. He was not a broad, speculative political thinker, did not suffer from the doubts and qualifications that always accompany such thought. His most abstract writing, "Presidential Problems," is perfectly concrete, though the questions treated in it would have been tempting to a discursive, imaginative philosopher. "It is a condition which confronts us — not a theory," is perhaps Cleveland's best-known saying. [56] He was always dealing with conditions, dealing with them fairly, honestly, but practically, and leaving theories on one side. The strong features of his character were all such as to give the conservative, negative element full force and vigor. He was simple and direct, and that helps. He was immensely silent, and that

167

helps. He had unlimited patience, and patience is as indispensable in conservatism as in other things. As he himself said, "Certainly the potency of patience as a factor in all worldly achievement and progress cannot be overestimated." [57] Finally he had determination pushed to a degree which he himself was perfectly ready to call obstinacy, "his native obstinacy, which he always insisted was his principal virtue." [58] He said on one occasion, "I want to tell you now that, if every other man in the country abandons this issue, I shall stick to it." [59] He said it and he meant it.

We have only to consider the chief historical events associated with Cleveland's name to see how marked in all of them is this negative element. I have already said that it was largely characteristic of his tariff activity. Negative, his effort to check the free coinage of silver. Negative, his superb action in the great railroad strike. Negative, essentially, even the most criticized of all his performances, the Venezuela message to Congress. As we look through his writings and those of his biographers, the thing that impresses us most overwhelmingly is veto, veto, veto. No doubt this is the chief function that all American constitutions leave to the executive. But in Cleveland's case it seems to have been exercised with temperamental readiness. Take his mayoralty, take his governorship, take his presidency: always the veto. His vetoes in four years amounted to "more than twice the number in the aggregate of all his predecessors," says Richardson. [60] And of course in no case was the motive mere opposition or petulance or personal grudge. Every veto was thought out with the most scrupulous care and justified with the most patient reasoning. The first functionary in the country sat up night after night till the small hours, studying why he should say no to the petty and insignificant petition of some fraudulent pensioner.

From one point of view there is infinite pathos in seeing a great statesman spend his soul on such minute detail of negation, instead of on the unsolved problems of the world. The ultimate value and fruitfulness of this negative attitude appears only when we consider that it was based upon the deepest, strongest, fundamental belief in the people and in popular government. For all his conservatism, Cleveland was no reactionary, no aristocrat, no advocate of ruling the masses by the assumed superior wisdom of a chosen few. He held that the people should rule themselves, that they could, and that they would, if a free chance was given them. He believed in American ideals, American traditions. He speaks of his "passionate Americanism," [61] and the phrase, coming from one who knew and swayed his passions, is immensely significant. And he believed in popular government because he put behind it the whole mass and solidity of his belief in God. God had ordained the framing of the American Republic. God sustained it. "A free people," he said, "without standards of right beyond what they saw or did, without allegiance to something unseen above them all, would soon sink below their own level." [62]

It was just because he believed heartily and wholly in American popular government that he wished to

169

guard it as it was. Let those who believed in neither
God nor man keep restlessly trying experiments, over-
turning the old without any assurance of the new.
He had studied the Constitution as the Fathers had
left it. He had seen it working and believed it would
work still. It might be imperfect, like other human
inventions. Would the new devices be less so? The
thing was, to take the old and treat it honestly, indus-
triously, faithfully. So treated, it would justify itself
in the future as it had done in the past.

Thus it was that as a superb negative force acting
for a great positive purpose Grover Cleveland did his
work in the world. A few grand phrases of his own
show how he did it better than any description I can
furnish. Speaking of Lincoln and his many military
pardons, he said: "Notwithstanding all that might
be objectionable in these, what was he doing? *He was
fortifying his own heart!* And that was his strength,
his own heart; *that* is a man's strength." [63] Fortifying his own heart! Again, there is the splendid sentence
about Secrteary Carlisle: "We are just right for each
other; he knows all I ought to know, *and I can bear
all we have to bear.*" [64] Could a man say it more
humbly and simply, "I can bear all I have to bear"?
Finally, there are almost the last words he ever uttered, and what finer last words could any human
being utter? "I have tried so hard to do right." [65]

A four-square, firm, solid, magnificent Titan, who
could speak the everlasting no, so rare and so essential in democracy. We still await the genius even
greater than he, who can speak the everlasting yes.

VII
HENRY JAMES

CHRONOLOGY

Henry James.
Born, New York City, April 15, 1843.
Educated in France and Switzerland and at
  Harvard Law School.
From 1869 lived mainly in England.
Roderick Hudson published, 1875.
Daisy Miller published, 1878.
The Portrait of a Lady published, 1881.
What Maisie Knew published, 1897.
The Ambassadors published, 1903.
The Golden Bowl published, 1904.
The American Scene published, 1907.
A Small Boy and Others published, 1913.
Became British subject, July 26, 1915.
Died, London, February 28, 1916.

HENRY JAMES

By J. S. Sargent, R.A.

VII

HENRY JAMES

I

HE was a man whose whole life was in art, and to whom life and art were inextricably one. He had no wife, he had no children, he had no country; for his flitting and vagrant cosmopolitan youth uprooted him from America, and, although the Great War impelled him at last to declare himself an English citizen, he had too much the habit of the wide world to become definitely identified with any particular nation. He lived and thought and felt to write great novels, and he wrote them, novels of an impossible subtlety and complexity, yet too beautiful and too original for men to let them die.

Of course all his art was based on life. He repeats and reiterates this. From an almost abnormally early age he began to study the faces and the hearts about him, to make notes, to register impressions, to accumulate material which might, somehow or other, sometime or other, serve his great and never-forgotten purpose. He was absolutely sincere in this. One of the great charms of his character in every aspect is sincerity and it is as evident in his art as in his daily living. He wanted truth and nothing else, to grasp it patiently and render it faithfully. "The novelist is a particular *window*, absolutely," he says, — "and of worth in so far as he is one." [1] And again, "I may therefore venture to say that the air of reality . . . seems to me to be the supreme virtue of a novel." [2] And yet again, more personally, "For myself I live, live intensely and am fed by life, and my value, whatever it be, is in my own kind of expression of that." [3]

He was always an acute, minute, tireless observer. He observed the external world constantly, and, though he was too busy with humanity to indulge often in long natural descriptions, he used delicate, fleeting touches to set human passion in just the background that will make it most impressive and most enthralling. He observed the outward frame of man with endless patient care and few have been more cunning in teasing it to yield its secrets. Above all, he observed the soul with curiosity and comprehension and even with tender sympathy, with awe and due, modest sense of the groping incompetence of the wisest, and perhaps he might have summed up his observation in the simple words of one of his characters, "Everything's terrible, cara — in the heart of man." [4]

Yet, for all this constant and searching observation, as one studies James, one gets an overwhelming sense that to him life was chiefly interesting, not in itself, but as matter for art. The crowding, shifting, shuddering turmoil of human existence was stuff to make novels of, or it was nothing. "All art is *expression*," he says, "and is thereby vividness." [5] But to him the expression was more than the thing expressed. Fact was crude, cumbrous, intrusive, perplexing. "More distinct and more numerous than I mostly *like* facts. . . . Nine tenths of the artist's interest in them is that of what he shall add to them and how he shall turn them." [6] Of his early youth, he tells us, "My face was turned from the first to the idea of representation — that of the gain of charm, interest, mystery, dignity, distinction, gain of importance in fine, on the part of the represented thing (over the thing of accident, of mere actuality, still unappropriated)." [7]

His object was always to make an exquisite, perfect work of art, and life must be fitted, moulded, transformed into a flawless achievement of ideal beauty; not the shallow beauty which eschews superficial ugliness, but the larger harmony which draws all threads and strands together into the final triumph of workmanship. Considerations extraneous to art, so-called moral aims and purposes, were to be discarded as merely distracting and inappropriate. It is true that few men ever lived with a finer or more delicate moral instinct, true also that moral motives and subtle questions of conduct often supplied the richest field for artistic disquisition. But again, these were only the material, interesting and valuable as furnishing stuff for the absorbing artistic passion to develop all its resources of cunning and cleverness. To teach lessons, to make the world better, this was not the artist's business, nor even was he bound to consider whether he might make it worse. Things beautiful ought not to make it worse, at any rate.

Not only did the intense preoccupation with artistic excellence shut out moral considerations; it even distracted thought from the vast variety and richness of life in general. It seems as if James, through all his long volumes, worked with bare soul and neglected the casual garb of circumstance, the outer trapping of profession and vocation, which differentiates souls to the eye of the more superficial observer. Balzac in his way, Trollope in his, produced a wide range of types, doctors, lawyers, preachers, workers in a dozen varied lines of human activity. There are few of these in James, and they appear only at moments, for some fleeting agency in the dramatic action. Generally speaking, also, he is confined to a limited social class, does not depict or care for the great ordinary herd which makes up the substance of humanity. I do not know of any more naïve confession of such spiritual exclusiveness than the sentence in the preface to the revised edition of "The Princess Casamassima": "We care, our curiosity and our sympathy care, comparatively little for what happens to the stupid, the coarse, and the blind; care for it, and for the effects of it, at the most as helping to precipitate what happens to the more deeply wondering, to the really sentient." [8] Yet the stupid, the coarse, and the blind make up the bulk of the world. Even if we presume to set ourselves above them, can we disregard them so completely?

There is no doubt that this detachment of Henry James from the crude facts of life was much fostered by his early and constant internationalism, his impersonal separation from all countries as such, not excepting his native America. One of his most ardent admirers declares that his chief mission was to civilize the United States. If so, it is to be feared that he did not greatly fulfil it. At any rate, America was a puzzle to him in earlier days, so far as he gave his thoughts to it at all; and when he came to study it in his old age, the puzzle was not diminished for him and certainly not for his readers. All the intense, crowding, sweating, grinding human complexity, which throbs from Boston to San Francisco, was mainly lost on him. It terrified him, dismayed him, was "stupid, coarse, blind," above all was too rough and violent to be fitted into nice, gauzy, shimmering webs of artistic achievement.

A striking illustration of this mighty predominance of the artistic attitude in James's temperament is that, keen as his powers of observing were, he was comparatively indifferent to fact as a matter of record, had not at least that sense of its sacredness which is inherent in the born historian. When he read the novels of his friends, he was not so much interested in them as they stood, but was busy always with the thought of rewriting them, making them over as they should have been in his artistic conception. His own past work he was not content to accept as a record of his own past self, to leave it to others as such a record; but in his old age he revised and altered with the most singular assiduity, producing, after all, a result, that was truly characteristic neither of his age nor of his youth. Matthew Arnold said, when reprinting some early writings, "Exactly as they stand, I should not have written them now, but perhaps they are none the worse on that account." [9] This was far from the attitude of James. Most curious of all, in publishing letters of his brother, he actually altered the text, alleging that what he saw fit to substitute was more characteristic than what his brother actually wrote. [10] And I do not know how the artist's claim to dominate crude fact can go farther than that.

So, although we must recognize that life and the study of life form the undeniable basis of James's, as of all other art, we constantly feel that with him the artistic instinct is so engrossing, so involving, that life is absorbed and smothered by it. There is analysis, endless analysis, inexhaustible analysis, reflection, dissection, connection, till a trifle seems drawn out to the end of the world. What other human being has more appreciated "the quite incalculable tendency of a mere grain of subject-matter to expand and develop and cover the ground when conditions happen to favor it"? [11] Nothing is left to stand out alone in vivid isolation and compelling brevity. The slightest motive is traced back into its roots and finest fibres, defined and refined, until it becomes at once monstrous and impalpable. The method is so subtle and elaborate that the trivial is made important by intense minuteness in the study of it and the very same minuteness makes the important trivial. Naturally this complication is least intrusive in the admirable short stories, and it took years to develop from the comparative clarity of "Roderick Hudson" to the extraordinary depths of "The Wings of the Dove" and "The Golden Bowl." But it is the mark of James's work everywhere and of his mind. He reveled in "shades" and again and again he enlarges on them. He reproaches

Bourget with the "love of intellectual daylight,"
which "is an injury to the patches of ambiguity and
the abysses of shadow which really are the clothing —
or much of it — of the *effects* that constitute the material of our trade." [12] His own characters grope in ambiguity and are garmented in shadow. He loved ghost
stories; but all his work is one great ghost story, with
the uneasy thrill, the teasing intensity of vagueness —
and the charm.

And here it must be insisted that never, never does
James's artistic passion degenerate into a mere mysti-
fication of words. He is as far as possible from the
tendency to disguise emptiness under phraseology
which is the plague of Browning. On the contrary,
words fail him, will not serve him, in the long, far pursuit of faint subtleties of distinction for which there
are no words. He strains words, forces them, loads
them with content past what their frail natures will
endure, and then still there is something beyond them
and him, shimmering, impalpable, which he strives to
feel and to make his reader feel, and cannot. The mere
verbalist in literature seeks to make nothing real, but
James's process is rather to refine away reality to
nothing.

And that which should give substance and structure
to this gelatinous mass of analysis, the secret of com-
position, simply betrays this passionate and conscientious artist still further. He has elaborate principles
and theories of order, of balance, of design; but they
are too elaborate and serve rather to increase the complication than to clarify it. He himself was fond of

insisting upon his dramatic instinct, maintained that he saw life in scenes and developed his stories largely upon a scenic method. Yet the dramatic theory, like the analytic, was excessive in its nature and rather deprived his work of sustained interest than informed it with breathing life. His plays, like his novels, are fascinatingly brilliant in detail: like the novels, they involve the reader in a labyrinth of shades from which there is no possible extrication. "It is art that *makes* life," he said; [13] and while there may be a sense in which this is profoundly true for all of us, life punished him by setting his great and original work apart from the thought of most persons whose real business is to live.

For there was never a more curious case of the intense, unselfish passion for art pushed so far as really to injure itself, to obscure itself by obscuring the material on which it works. To refine, to distinguish, to conjure up problems for the mere pleasure of solving them — these are different tastes from the passion for life as such. "You see what a mistake you'd make to see abysses of subtlety in my having been merely natural," says one of James's own characters. [14] She might have said it to her creator. "I *love* life—in art, though I hate it anywhere else," says another. [15] And it would not be fair to say this of her creator unrestrictedly, but there would be a certain point in it. Far more significant and suggestive, in fact of a singular weight and significance for James's whole work, is his cruel phrase about himself: "And I find our art, all the while, more difficult of practice, and want, with that, to do it in a more and more difficult way; it being really, at bottom, only difficulty that interests me. Which is a most accursed way to be constituted." [16]

II

DID the man, then, you ask, have no life of his own, aside from his absorbing preoccupation with art? It is surprising how little, as far as the records that we have inform us. No doubt these records are limited. The two volumes of delightful letters, recently published, belong to the writer's mature and later life and naturally show more of reflection than passion. The three volumes of autobiography also were written in old age, and in such a temperament it was inevitable that thoughts should be more remembered than feelings. Yet even so in a history of boyhood one would expect some outburst of hearty and violent experience, and there is none, none: just an endless chain of subtle analyses of petty facts, the vast dissection of "a case" like "the cases" of the novels, in which all petulant, vivid assertion of personality is drowned, absorbed, in shades, refinements, complications, connections, without stint or limit. There is at times the vague intimation of longing to live, of regret for not having lived. Surely there is something personal to the author in the words of Strether in "The Ambassadors": "Live all you can; it's a mistake not to. . . . I was either, at the right time, too stupid or too intelligent to have it [the illusion of freedom], and now I'm a case of reaction against the mistake." [17] Further, there is the insistence that the artist must live to accumulate his stock in trade: "We must know, as much as possible, in our beautiful art, yours and mine, what we are talking about — and the only way to know is to have lived and loved and cursed and floundered and enjoyed and suffered. I think I don't regret a single 'excess' of my responsive youth — I only regret in my chilled age, certain occasions and possibilities I did n't embrace." [18] And this does sound like the thrill of human existence. But I am inclined to set against it the words to Howells, "such fine primitive passions *lose* themselves for me in the act of contemplation, or at any rate in the act of reproduction." [19] Since the weight of evidence goes to show that for this intensely concentrated spirit, in youth as well as in age, contemplation, profound inward absorption was the essence of life, and I find endless significance in the revealing phrase of William James as to his younger brother, when scarcely out of boyhood, "Never did I see a so-much uninterested creature in the affairs of those about him." [20]

Let us consider him in relation to the common concerns of men and see how much alive he was. Sport, athletics, exercise? None whatever, even in the sporting years. Though he was of a nervous, anxious temperament, nothing in his physique would seem to have cut him off from bodily activity. But no aspect of it appears to have interested him, and none enters into his novels.

Money, business? He was frugal and self-controlled in his own expenditure, wisely liberal as regards others. He would have liked to make money from his work for a little more amplitude of living. But money as an object in life he abhorred, and the business man, as a type, including in his fancy most of his American fellow-citizens, was as monotonous as he was detestable.

Even books, reading, were of minor importance, except those that bore directly upon his own pursuit. He does indeed say that "reading tends to take for me the place of experience,"[21] and he at times expresses enthusiasm for it. Beyond doubt, he was intimately familiar with the works of modern novelists. But the great writers of the past, even the imaginative writers, do not figure largely in his life.

Nor does it seem that he thought widely or curiously. His father was a subtle metaphysician, his brother an active and creative one. Henry watched their lucubrations rather helplessly and very indifferently. Science interested him no more than metaphysics. The great physical discoveries of the age he lived in left him without enthusiasm. On all these personal points the evidence of the novels must, of course, be used with caution. But the utter absence of broad intellectual movement in them only supports the testimony of the letters and autobiographies. It is true that this concrete attitude toward life, coupled with the tendency to dissolve the spirit in endless shades and complications, produced a singular respect and awe in face of the individual soul and its independent existence. This is what James's secretary, Miss Bosanquet, means, when she calls his novels "a sustained and passionate plea for the fullest freedom of the individual development that he saw continually imperiled by barbarian stupidity." [22] But if he respected the soul, he did not care to philosophize about it. Even as to his own art, which he discusses so often and so acutely, the discussion is more apt to be concerned with the concrete than with philosophical aspects. "Thank God," he says, "I've no *opinions*. . . . I'm more and more only aware of things as a more or less mad panorama, phantasmagoria and dime museum." [23]

This comment was, indeed, made in regard to politics, although its significance is far more than political. As to public affairs, James's indifference, until his very last years, was mainly sovereign. Here his internationalism appears as both cause and effect. A man who has no country is not likely to be intensely patriotic. A man who cares little for the history of the past is not likely to be much aroused over the social and political movements of the present. "I fear I am too lost in the mere spectacle for any decent morality," he says. [24] Even the spectacle interested him more as embodied in individuals than as affecting great masses of men.

With religion it was much as with other abstract motives. James himself confesses that he had little contact with practical religion in his youth, and it is obvious that he had little interest in it in age. His spiritual attitude is perhaps as well summed up in the following passage as anywhere. "I don't know *why* we live — the gift of life comes to us from I don't know what source or for what purpose; but I believe we can go on living for the reason that (always of course up to a certain point) life is the most valuable thing we know

anything about." [25] Of prayer he says, "I don't pray
in general, and don't understand it." [26] Of a future life
he says, "It takes one whole life—for some persons, at
least *dont je suis*—to learn how to live at all; which is
absurd if there is not to be another in which to apply the
lesson." [27] Of Balzac, whom he so greatly admired, he
says: "His sincere, personal beliefs may be reduced to
a very compact formula; he believed that it was possible to write magnificent novels, and that he was the
man to do it." [28] Again, "Of what is to be properly
called religious feeling we do not remember a suggestion
in all his many pages." [29] I do not know why these
words cannot be aptly applied to Henry James.

We may indeed appreciate keenly the lack in others
of what we lack ourselves. In "The American Scene"
James expresses with the utmost vigor the religious deficiencies of his countrymen: "The field of American
life is as bare of the Church as a billiard table of a
centre-piece; a truth that the myriad little structures
'attended' on Sundays and on the 'off' evenings of
their 'sociables' proclaim as with the audible sound of
the roaring of a million mice." [30] But the complaint
here is rather æsthetic than devotional, and the
æsthetic side of religion was what touched James most.
Yet it is extremely curious to note that even his æsthetic
enjoyments were dwarfed and dulled by the absorbing
passion of creative analysis. Again, speaking of Balzac,
he remarks his lack of appreciation of the beauty of the
world and explains it by saying that "Balzac was as
little as possible of a poet." [31] And as before one feels
that James was as little as possible of a poet also. Ex-

ternal nature, when touched at all in his novels and in his letters, is touched, like everything else, with extreme and fine imaginative delicacy. But there is rarely any indication of rapture about it. In art he was familiar with great painting and at times shows a deep interest in it. He adored Italy for its artistic richness, for its depth of memory, and for its melancholy associative beauty. But outside of painting he does not seem to have cared much for the simply beautiful. His pleasure in poetry was limited. He never wrote it and seldom read it, unless certain French writers. Music was a sealed world to him.

It is when we come to human relations that James as a man really begins to seem alive. To be sure, like most intellectual workers, he lived much in solitude and cherished it, sought again and again to find some remote corner of the world where he could order and develop his crowding visions without the bustling intrusion of critics or flatterers or even friends. Yet in the main he enjoyed people, enjoyed frequenting society and dining out, haunting the thick throng for the inspiration and stimulus it gave his curious spirit. He sighs in age over the social ideal of his youth: "The waltz-like, rhythmic rotation from great country-house to great country-house, to the sound of perpetual music and the acclamation of the 'house-parties' that gather to await you." [32] His conversation was delightful, full of wit, color, suggestion, a trifle moderate and elaborate, like his writing, but rich with succulence and charm. "When he could not get the very word or adjective he wanted, it was most amusing to

see him with one hand in the air, till he found it, when
he flashed his hand down into the palm of the other and
brought with a triumphant look the word he wanted,
the exact word." [33] And his talk, like his books, and
like the whole man himself, was always sincere: earnest, scrupulous, and winning in its sincerity. The noble, thoughtful, kindly face alone was enough to make
a friend of you.

How I should like to get some glimpse of Henry
James in love! But this side of his life is completely
hidden from us. He makes no allusion to it in the autobiography and there is no hint of it in his letters. Yet
his novels are saturated with love, contain, in fact,
little or nothing else, though it is love quintessenced
and alembicated till it hardly knows itself. One would
suppose that there was plenty of it in his life. And his
love-letters would have been one of the curiosities of literature. Fancy the subtleties, the spiritual doublings,
the harassing doubts and questions and qualifications!
Yet this may be all wrong, and actual, absorbing love
might have simplified and clarified his soul beyond anything else on earth. Who can say? Unless some woman
still lives who has some of those letters. All that comes
to us is the lovely, searching, pathetic suggestion in six
words, "the starved romance of my life." [34]

What we do know and actually see and hear is the
depth of his tenderness and devotion to his family and
friends, though even this warm and rushing stream does
at times risk extinction in the huge quagmire of his
haunting analysis. Hear him enlarge on the word
"liking," and wonder at him: "The process represented

by that word was for each of us, I think, a process so involved with other operations of the spirit, so beautifully complicated and deformed by them, that our results in this sort doubtless eventually lost themselves in the labyrinth of our reasons." [35] And well they might; but fortunately they did n't. I know no letters more filled with a penetrating, involving affection. This love, he admits, counts for more in the world than even art, though he admits it grudgingly: "You are precious to literature—but she is precious to the affections, which are larger, yet in a still worse way." [36] When those he loves are absent, he longs for them with a hungry longing which nothing else can satisfy, longs for news of them, longs for words of solicitude and thoughts of tenderness. In spite of his brother's youthful charge of lack of interest, he enters into their joys and triumphs. He enters into their griefs and sufferings also, and with a comprehension and sweetness and tact of sympathy which must have been infinitely helpful. I cannot omit the earnest, frank, wise, noble words which he addressed to one he loved, in a great sorrow. Nothing marks more the real depth of humanity hidden in him under the apparently indifferent surface: "Only sit tight yourself *and go through the movements of life.* That keeps up our connection with life — I mean of the immediate and apparent life; behind which, all the while, the deeper and darker and unapparent, in which things *really* happen to us, learns, under that hygiene, to stay in its place. Let it get out of its place and it swamps the scene; besides which its place, God knows, is enough for it! Live it all through, every inch of it — out of it something valuable will come—but live it ever so quietly." [37]

So it seems that the whole personal life of James, aside from his art, centered in simple human affection. And the flower of this affection was his passionate interest in the Great War. I do not think he was much concerned with the political and moral questions involved. He rarely discusses or refers to them, and such things never had interested him before. But those he loved were suffering, those whom his friends loved were suffering, humanity was suffering. And all the depths of tenderness, which lay always, not smothered, but eclipsed, forgotten, at the bottom of his heart, was called into intense, active, beneficent energy. If it had not been for those terrible years, something would have been missing, not to his character, for it was there deep hidden all along, but to our understanding and appreciation of his character. He was always a great writer, but the war revealed him to every one as a most lovable man.

III

YET, after all, his real humanity, his essential, vivid, passionate existence, was in his art, and it is most curious to watch him living perfectly in the exercise of that, when he was so largely oblivious to everything else. "What's art but an intense life — if it be real?" says one of his characters. [38] The art of Henry James was an intense life, at any rate.

All his days he labored at it and much of his nights was given to new developments, new inventions, new and vaster analysis. The taking of notes was his business. He took notes on pleasure and pain, on suffering and hope, notes on any casual incident of life, notes on his family, on his friends, on himself. "If one was to undertake to tell tales," he says, "and to report with truth on the human scene, it could be but because 'notes' had been from the cradle the ineluctable consequence of one's greatest inward energy." [39] In this close and unremitting effort there was, of course, a large amount of ambition, of desire for direct and obvious success, but it was also a matter of instinct, of a habit of life which with daily exercise grew ever more exacting and more tyrannous.

And it was not only the formal daily habit, the rooted necessity of accomplishing a definite task at a definite hour. There was a splendid glow and thrill of excitement in the work. External stimulus might help, the commendation of friends, the enthusiasm of admirers, even the stinging of captious critics. But the external was often more annoying than helpful. "I wince even at eulogy, and I wither (for exactly 2 minutes and $\frac{1}{2}$) at any qualification of adulation." [40] What really counted was the rushing, the inexplicable artistic impetus itself. Why should a weary soul toil and strain to make a troop of shadows strut and fret and vex themselves for an hour and then fade utterly? Who knows? But James did it with devouring passion, like so many others. And the decay of age and the wretched debility of the body did not diminish one jot the fury of creative hope. At sixty-five he writes: "I never have had such a sense of almost bursting, late in the day though it be, with violent and lately too much repressed creative ... intention." [41]

And of course triumph and success, when they came, as they did come in even James's remote, perplexed, and unpopular career, were acceptable, were welcome. To what artist are they not? "Daisy Miller has been, as I have told you before, a really quite extraordinary hit," [42] and such hits do tickle the heart that is most detached. But the best glory — perhaps — is the feeling of secure achievement, and the best commendation is one's own: "The thing carries itself to my maturer and gratified sense as with every symptom of soundness, an insolence of health and joy." [43]

The mischief of it is that this splendid exultation in what one has accomplished does not, cannot last. There are the difficulties of accomplishing anything. There are the external difficulties, the horrid plague of printers and publishers, interruptions, distractions. There are the internal difficulties, still worse, when inspiration simply stops and one sits and stares and longs and does nothing and gets nowhere. Moreover, no critic, however captious, sees one's defects so clearly and overpoweringly as one sees them one's self. One sees them so well, is so cuttingly aware of the weak points, that on dark days it seems as if the work was all weak points and nothing else.

And then come depression and discouragement, even in a buoyant soul, and James, as he himself admits, had a soul to which anxiety and dread came far too easily. He is depressed if he is prevented from working. When he begins a piece of work, he is haunted by "a nervous fear that I shall not have enough of my peculiar tap to 'go round.'" [44] And again, "To finish a book in quiet and to begin another in fear." [45] While the completion is really as agitating as the commencement: "always ridden by a superstitious terror of not finishing, for finishing's and for the precedent's sake, what I have begun." [46] And for those who look upon authorship as an ecstasy, he has this general comment, which is certainly not exhilarating: "The profession of delight has always struck me as the last to consort, for the artist, with any candid account of his troubled effort — ever the sum, for the most part, of so many lapses and compromises, simplifications and surrenders." [47]

Also, however indifferent one may be to the commendation of the general public, the sense of failure is wearing, blighting to any mortal man. And it cannot be denied that, as regards the reading world at large, failure was the usual lot of Henry James. Works rejected, works accepted and delayed indefinitely in publication, works published and then treated with careless indifference, bringing little praise and less profit — when these torment the beginner in literature, he may remember that they also tormented the greatest of American novelists.

Nothing epitomizes better James's struggle and effort, his gleams of hope and success, and his complete lack of it in the grosser sense, than his dealings with the theatre. He did not turn his attention to the stage till comparatively late in life, and therefore there was always the consolation that if he had begun younger he could have accomplished more. But when the fever seizes him, he is convinced that at last he has found his proper sphere and that the drama is the real medium in which his genius should achieve its destined working. "The strange thing is that I always, universally, knew *this* was my more characteristic form — but was kept away from it by a half-modest, half-exaggerated sense of the difficulty . . . of the conditions. But now that I have accepted them and met them, I see that one isn't at all, needfully, their victim, but is, from the moment one *is* anything, one's self, worth speaking of, their master." [48] And he sets himself to be the master triumphantly. He toils more than he ever dreamed of toiling on fiction. He studies the secrets of technique with which those who_think they understand the theatre have beguiled so many passionate aspirants. He has his moments of hope, of confidence, of enthusiasm, and portrays them with his customary vividness. A fairly successful provincial performance cheers him, encourages him. "The passage from knock-kneed nervousness (the night of the *première*, as one clings in the wings, to the curtain rod, as to the *pied des autels*) to a simmering serenity is especially life-saving in its effect." [49] Then things go wrong and hope yields to utter disgust. And again, after one failure, after two failures, a word of praise, a trifle of alluring temptation, seduce him to renewed, more strenuous effort. But the end is fatal, inevitable, as it has been for so many whom that fascinating siren has betrayed to far more complete destruction. Actors are patronizing, encroaching, tyrannous, ignorant. Audiences are more tyrannous and more ignorant still.

Let us leave the loathed stage and go back to the quiet writing of profound, great fiction, where at least the failure is that of indifference and not of audible contempt.

Through all this theatrical convulsion a common pretext with James was that he needed money and that the theatre was a dazzlingly facile and convenient means of getting it. All he cared to give to the stage was "time to dig out eight or ten rounded masterpieces and make withal enough money to enable me to retire in peace and plenty for the unmolested business of a *little* supreme writing as distinguished from gouging." [50] Alas, the stage was no more fruitful than other things in this direction, and it is really pitiful to see that such enormous labor and such admirable genius could produce no more tangible pecuniary result. But it is clear enough that, though money might be the pretext, the passion went far deeper than money. Success, triumph, applause, in one simple word, glory, were underlying motives with James, as with all other artists. He longed, not only to do great things, but to have the seal of immediate wonder and enthusiasm set upon them. And in spite of the approval of many of the discerning, few writers who have toiled so vastly and worthily have received less of universal recognition.

The fine, the most notable thing through all this comparative failure is the largeness, the sweetness, the dignity of James's attitude. Such public neglect of a man's work is apt to produce sourness and bitterness. With him it did not. Criticism he considered thoughtfully and estimated wisely. It did not, indeed, often affect his aims or methods. When does it ever? But he showed a large charity in entering into the intention of the critic, was always ready to allow for other points of view than his own. Nor did he often fall into the error of so many disappointed authors, that of railing against the taste of his contemporaries. He could not always resist some rebellion against the triumph of the mediocre, could not accept the vogue of the obviously cheap and tawdry. But in the main he feels that he writes for the few and with the discerning commendation of the few he must be satisfied. And his are the admirable words of rebuke to those who would revenge their ill-success upon the world about them: "Most forms of contempt are unwise; but one of them seems to us peculiarly ridiculous — contempt for the age one lives in." [51] Broad kindliness, thoughtful, earnest, patient sincerity, these are not always the distinguishing qualities of the artist; in James they were eminently and charmingly exemplified.

In nothing perhaps more than in his tone toward his fellow-writers. Here again pretentious emptiness sometimes wins deserved condemnation. But in the main he was largely generous and sympathetic. He had many close friends among the authors of his time, friends to whom he wrote with the peculiar exquisite tenderness of friendship that characterizes his letters. Many of these friends were much younger than he and many of them quickly passed him in the race for success and financial profit. He never resented this, never showed any small soreness or grudging. He counseled wisely and congratulated warmly and cherished an ever-growing affection where in many rivalry would have fostered a certain chilliness, if not estrangement. Few things of the kind are more touching and pleasing than his manly, simple acceptance of the unnecessary and ill-mannered criticism introduced by his near friend Mr. Wells into his novel "Boon." [52]

So the long, patient, toilsome life flitted away, leaving a huge mass of production behind it, which, after all, had perhaps not greatly affected the busy world. But with all the toil and all the struggle and all the disappointment, few writers have got more substantial satisfaction out of the mere doing of their own work. The mystery of words and their strange, subtle, creative and created relation to thoughts has not been fully elucidated yet and perhaps never will be. But it is certain that, for the born worker in them, they have inexplicable and inexhaustible secrets and sources of delight and joy. Who is there who has probed these secrets and drained these sources more passionately than Henry James?

VIII
JOSEPH JEFFERSON

CHRONOLOGY

Joseph Jefferson.

Born, Philadelphia, February 20, 1829.

Acted at Franklin Theatre, New York, 1837.

Married Margaret Clements Lockyer, May 19, 1850.

Made hit as Dr. Pangloss, August 31, 1857.

In Australia, 1861–1865.

Appeared as Rip Van Winkle at the Adelphi Theatre, London, September 4, 1865.

Married Sarah Isabel Warren, December 20, 1867.

Produced *The Rivals* at the Arch Street Theatre, Philadelphia, 1880.

Published *Autobiography*, 1889–1890.

All-Star *Rivals* Tour, 1896.

Died, Palm Beach, Florida, April 23, 1905.

JOSEPH JEFFERSON

VIII

JOSEPH JEFFERSON

I

JEFFERSON was not born on the stage, but his family for generations had been associated with the theatre. His first appearance that he remembered was in 1832, when he was three years old, and he continued to act in all sorts of parts and with all sorts of experiences almost till his death in 1905. The theatrical influence and atmosphere seemed to surround him at all times. He grew up with the strange richness of wandering Bohemian vagrancy which attaches to the profession in the dreams of youth, and he met his full share of the hard knocks and bitter struggles which the dreams of youth pass over lightly. Also, he had something of the easy, gracious temper which enjoys the charms of such a life and takes the trials as they come. His father had even more of it. When he was reduced to total bankruptcy, he went fishing, and said to those who found him so occupied: "I have lost everything, and I am so poor now that I really cannot afford to let anything worry me." [1] The son inherited from his mother a soul of somewhat more substantial tissue. He did not like bankruptcy and avoided it. Yet even he thoroughly savored a nomad life and a changing world. He writes of such: "It had a roving, joyous, gipsy kind of attraction in it that was irresistible." [2]   It is said that his great-grandmother died laughing. [3]   He lived laughing, at any rate, or smiling, with the tenderest sympathy, at all the strange vagaries of existence. To be sure of it, you need only study his portraits, that curiously wrinkled face, which seems as if generations of laughter had kneaded it to the perfect expression of all pathos and all gayety

The striking thing is that, with this profuse contact with every side of human experience, which must have included the basest, the most sordid, the most vicious, the man should have kept his own nature high and pure to a singular degree. Certainly no one was more in the world, and in a sense of the world; yet few have remained more unspotted by it. He often quoted with approval the fine saying, "We cannot change the world, but we can keep away from it." [4] He kept away from it in spirit. His great friend, President Cleveland, said of him: "Many knew how free he was from hatred, malice, and uncharitableness, but fewer knew how harmonious his qualities of heart, and mind, and conscience blended in the creation of an honest, upright, sincere, and God-fearing man." [5] And Colonel Watterson, who was intimately acquainted with him, remarks, more specifically: "I never knew a man whose moral sensibilities were more acute. He loved the respectable. He detested the unclean." [6]

This moral tone was not simply the sanity of a wholesome, well-adjusted nature; it was a delicacy, an instinctive refinement that rejected the subtler shades of coarseness as well as mere brutality. Not that Jefferson was the least in the world of a Puritan. The suggestion would be laughable. But he avoided the obscene as he avoided the ugly. He disliked grossness on the stage as he disliked it in the drawing-room, and even deliberately asserted that the latter should be a criterion for the former, [7] which is perhaps going a little far. And he wanted as much decency behind the scenes as before. "Booth's theatre," he said, "is conducted as a theatre should be — like a church behind the curtain and like a counting-house in front of it." [8]

He not only avoided the moral looseness of Bohemianism; he could not tolerate its easy-going indifference to artistic method. He reflected deeply and carefully on the nature of his art and did not cease to reflect on it as long as he practised it. He had definite views as to its purpose, and, while we may not agree with those views, we must at least recognize their validity for one of Jefferson's temperament. Realism he would have nothing to do with. Art, he urged, was from its very nature selective, suggestive, aimed to give the spiritual essence, not the superficial, material detail. Just so far as these details served the spirit, they were to be used and developed amply; but they were to be disregarded altogether, when they threatened to drag down the spirit and smother it.

He gave careful attention to the audience and its point of view. The strength of his artistic achievement lay both in distinction and in human feeling, but with the emphasis rather on human feeling, and he knew it and studied the human hearts to which he addressed himself. All the human hearts, moreover. He was no actor to evening dress and diamonds. How admirable is his appeal to Miss Shaw to remember the second balcony: "They are just as much entitled to hear and see and enjoy as are the persons in the private boxes." [9]

And he reflected and often spoke on the great critical problem of whether the actor should act from feeling or from intellect. To Jefferson's keen common sense the problem was hardly a problem at all. Every actor must use feeling and intellect both, the proportion differing according to the temperament. An intense imaginative sympathy with the emotion of the character involved must lie at the bottom of every successful impersonation. But this imaginative sympathy must at all times be controlled by clear and competent analysis. Surely no actor could have had keener sensibilities than had Jefferson himself. Once, at a pathetic moment in a part he had played over and over again, he was observed to falter, lost himself, and the curtain fell abruptly. "I broke down," he explained afterwards, "completely broke down. I turned away from the audience to recover myself. But I could not and had the curtain rung." [10] Yet he was commonly self-possessed enough in the most intense situations to make comments to his fellow-actors, and he summed up the whole question in the often-quoted saying, "For myself, I know that I act best when the heart is warm and the head is cool." [11]

As Jefferson was thorough in analyzing the theory of his profession, so he was industrious and conscientious in the practice of it. Although, in his later years, he confined himself to a few parts, he had been in his youth an actor of wide range, and he never ceased to study his oft-repeated triumphs for new effects and possibilities, was never the man to lie back upon established reputation and forget the toil necessary to sustain it. " I learn something about my art every night," he said, even in old age. [12] And he not only worked, but he worked with method and foresight. He suggests in his "Autobiography" that he was careless and unreliable as to facts, [13] and perhaps he was in indifferent matters. But when it came to planning a campaign, he knew what he was seeking and got it. For he was an excellent man of business. So many actors earn great sums and let them slip through their fingers. Not Jefferson. His ideas of financial management were broad and liberal. He put no spite into it and no meanness. See his excellent remarks on competition and opposition. [14] Nor did he desire money for itself. A moderate income is enough for him. "Less than this may be inconvenient at times; more than this is a nuisance." [15] But hard lessons had taught him the value of a dollar when he saw it, the pleasure it would give and the misery it would save, and when the dollars came, he held on to them.

In his relations with his fellow-actors he appears to have been delightful. At least I have looked rather widely for fault-finding and have not discovered it. He enjoyed practical jokes, as in the case of the exquisitely dressed dandy whom he had to embrace upon the stage: "I held him tight and rumpled his curls, and then I heard him murmur, in a tone of positive agony, 'Oh, God!' He was not in the least hurt, but he seemed to feel that his last hour had come." [16] No doubt

Jefferson was tolerant of such jokes when played upon him. Also, with his charming frankness, he lays bare in himself the weaknesses to which human nature is liable. Jealousy? "In this instance my rival was a good actor, but not too good to be jealous of me, and if our positions had been reversed the chances are that I would have been jealous of him." [17] Temper? He had temper and showed it, as he illustrates by various examples, without excusing himself. Quarrels? They occurred in his life, as in most lives, and he admits that his part in them was not always creditable. But the quarrels were relieved and soon healed by a wide comprehension of the human heart and love of it. And, above all, a sane philosophy taught that no quarrel should be perpetuated by talking about it or making any parade of it whatever. "If people could only realize how little the public care for the private quarrels of individuals — except to laugh at them — they would hesitate before entering upon a newspaper controversy." [18] If Whistler could have learned that lesson, his life would have been pleasanter to read about.

And Jefferson's good terms with his fellows were by no means confined to the negative. He was always ready for a frolic with them. He was cordially interested in their affairs. He was willing to give both money and time to extricate them from difficulties. He could do what is perhaps even harder, bestow unstinted and discerning praise upon their achievements. And he could stand up for their professional dignity, whether they were alive or dead. When a fashionable minister refused to perform the funeral service for an actor on account of his calling, Jefferson asked in wrath if there was no church where he could get it done. "There is a little church around the corner," was the reply. "Then, if this be so, God bless 'the little church around the corner.'" [19] The name sticks to this day. No wonder that a friend who knew him intimately could write, "He was the most lovable person I had ever met either in or out of my profession." [20]

A better test than even relations with the profession generally is that of management of the actors in his own company and under his especial charge. It is evident that he preserved discipline. Irregularities in conduct and irregularities in artistic method he would not tolerate. But he was reasonable in discipline, and he was gentle, as gentle, we are told, with his subordinates as with his children and grandchildren. [21] In strong contrast to actors like Macready and Forrest, he had the largest patience in meeting unexpected difficulties. One night the curtain dropped in the midst of a critical scene. Jefferson accepted the situation with perfect calmness. Afterwards he inquired the cause of the trouble, and one of the stage-hands explained that he had leaned against the button that gave the signal. "Well," said Jefferson, "will you kindly find some other place to lean to-morrow night?" [22]

He was helpful to those about him, and gave advice and encouragement when needed, but this was less by constant lecturing than by the force and suggestion of his own example. You could not be with him without learning, if you had one atom of the stuff of success in you. Some great artists daunt and discourage by their very presence. Jefferson soothed. When he saw that you were anxious and troubled, "he laid his hand on your shoulder in that gentle way that stilled all tumult in one and made everything easy and possible, saying: 'It will be all right.'" [23]

It is true that some urged and do still that Jefferson wanted all the stage and all the play to himself. At a certain point in his career he became a star. After that he altered plays to suit his own prominence and at last centred practically his whole effort on a very inferior piece that happened to be adapted to his temperament and gave him enormous professional success. It may reasonably be argued that this desire to engross attention to himself kept him out of real masterpieces, and even more subtly that he had not the genius to make himself unquestioned master of those masterpieces. On the other hand, his admirers insist that, before he became a one-part actor, he appeared in a great variety of parts, over a hundred in all, and in most, competently, if not triumphantly. There is no doubt that he himself felt the charges of repetition and self-assertion, though he could always meet them with his charming humor, as when he tells the story of his friends' giving him a Christmas present of "The Rivals" with all the parts but his own cut out. [24] The cleverest thing he ever said as to the lack of variety was his answer to Matthews, who charged him with making a fortune with one part and a carpet-bag. "It is perhaps better to play one part in different ways than to play many parts all in one way." [25] And Winter's defence against egotism is probably in the main justified: "When he was on the stage he *liked* to be the centre of attention; he liked to have the whole scene to himself; but he perfectly well knew the importance of auxiliaries and the proportion of component parts to make up a symmetrical whole; he could, and when needful, he always did completely subordinate himself to the requirements of the scene." [26]

But by far the most interesting light on Jefferson's view of his own professional methods is to be found in the conversation reported by Miss Mary Shaw as to her performance of Gretchen in "Rip Van Winkle." Miss Shaw had been inclined to emphasize the possibilities of tenderness in Gretchen's character, but Jefferson, in his infinitely gentle way, put a stop to this immediately. "You must not once during the play, except in the last act, call the attention of the audience to any ordinary rule of conduct or mode of feeling. You must play everything with the idea of putting forth this central figure Rip Van Winkle, as more and more lovable, the more and more he outrages the sensibilities, that being the ethical meaning of the play." [27] And there are many other words to the same effect, all admirably ingenious and on the whole reasonable. Only I should like to have seen Jefferson smile, as he said them.

Whether he smiled, or whether he was serious, there can be no doubt that, with all his gentleness and all his humor, he had an immense ambition that stuck by him till he died. Over and over again he acknowledges this, with his graceful jesting, which covers absolute sincerity: "As the curtain descended the first night on that remarkably successful play ["Our American Cousin"], visions of large type, foreign countries, and increased remuneration floated before me, and I resolved to be a star if I could." [28] Those who think only of his later glory do not realize the long years of difficulty and struggle. His youth knew the plague of fruitless effort. He met hunger and cold, deception and rejection. His words about failure have the vividness of intimate acquaintance with the subject. "If you are unsuccessful as a poet, a painter, an architect, or even a mechanic, it is only your work that has failed; but with the actor it does not end here: if he be condemned, it is himself that has failed." [29] And further, "The mortification of a personal and public slight is so hard to bear that he casts about for any excuse rather than lay the blame upon himself." [30] Stage-fright, utter distrust of genius and fortune, — he knew it, oh, how well he knew it! To the very end he was nervous over the chance of some sudden incapacity or untoward accident. "I am always attacked with a nervous fit when I am to meet a new assemblage of actors and actresses." [31] And he said to an amateur who asked him for a cure for such feelings, "If you find one, I wish you would let me have it." [32]

He was as sensitive to applause and appreciation as to failure. When words of approval began to come, they were drunk in with eagerness. "How anxious I used to be in the morning to see what the critic said, quickly scanning the article and skipping over the praise of the other actors, so as to get to what they said about me." [33] And years did not abate the zest or dull the edge of it. To be sure, he liked discretion in compliments, as did Doctor Johnson, who said to Hannah More, "Madam, before you flatter a man so grossly to his face, you should consider whether your flattery is worth his having." Jefferson's method was gentler. To a lady who hailed him as "You dear, great man!" he answered, "Madam, you make me very uncomfortable." [34] But when the compliments were deftly managed, he liked them. "He was susceptible to honest admiration," says Mr. Wilson. "I have often heard him declare since, that he would not give the snap of his finger for anybody who was not." [35] And when the compliment came, not from an individual, but from a vast audience, he found it uplifting, exhilarating beyond most things on earth. This stimulus was so splendid, so out of normal experience, that, with his mystical bent, he was inclined to relate it to some magnetic agency. "He claimed," says Miss Shaw, "that what he gave the audience in nervous force, in artistic effort, in inspiration, he received back in full measure, pressed down and running over. . . . And how well I saw this great truth demonstrated by Mr. Jefferson. Every night this delicate old man, after having been virtually on the stage every moment for hours in a play he had acted for thirty-seven years, and which therefore of itself afforded him little or no inspiration, would come off absolutely refreshed instead of exhausted." [36]

Few human beings have had more opportunity to drink the cup of immediate triumph to the bottom. Jefferson himself often enlarged upon the ephemeral quality of the actor's glory. No doubt the thought of this gave added poignancy to his rendering of the celebrated phrase in "Rip Van Winkle," "Are we so soon forgot when we are gone!" [37] And he urged that it was but just that this glory, being so brief, should be immense and fully savored. He savored it, with perfect appreciation of its casual elements, but still he savored it with large and long delight. He recognized fully that his lot had been fortunate, and that, although he had had to toil for success, he had achieved it. "I have always been a very contented man whatever happened," he said, "and I think I have had good reason to be." [38] He recognized also in his triumph the substantial quality which comes from normal growth; as he beautifully phrased it, "that sweet and gradual ascent to good fortune that is so humanizing." [39] Respect, tenderness, appreciation, from young and old, rich and poor, wise and unwise, flowed about his ripe age and mellowed it, and he acknowledged them again and again in most touching words. "It has been dear to me — this life of illuminated emotion — and it has been so magnificently repaid. . . . I have been doubly repaid by the sympathetic presence of the people when I was playing, and the affection that seems to follow me, like the sunshine streaming after a man going down the forest trail that leads over the hills to the lands of morning. No, I can't put it in words." [40] Then he added, with the whimsical turn which gave his talk so much of its charm, "Perhaps it's a good thing to quit the stage before the people have a chance to change their minds about me." [41]

JOSEPH JEFFERSON

As is well known, the climax of Jefferson's fortunate career lay in the discovery of "Rip Van Winkle," not of course as a new play, but as something perfectly suited to Jefferson himself. His whole account of this discovery, of the first suggestion on a haymow in a country barn on a rainy day, of the gradual growth of the piece and its final triumph, is extremely curious. [42] Equally curious is the study of the play itself. As read, it appears to be crude, inept, inadequate, illiterate. It is not that the language is simple. Much of it is not simple, but heavily, commonly pretentious, with that conventionality which is as foreign to life as it is to good writing. Yet Jefferson took this infirm, tottering patch of literary ineptitude and by sheer artistic skill made it a human masterpiece. When the play was first produced in England, Boucicault, the author, expressed his doubts as to Jefferson's handling of it: "Joe, I think you are making a mistake: you are shooting over their heads." Jefferson answered: "I'm not even shooting at their heads — I'm shooting at their hearts." [43] He did not miss his mark.

II

So much for the actor. In studying him we have had glimpses of the man, but he deserves to be developed much more fully. First, as to intelligence. His shrewdness, his keenness, his acute insight into life and human nature appear in every record of him. He understood men and women, read their tempers, their desires, their hopes and fears; no doubt largely by his own, as is the surest way. For he made a constant, careful, and

211

clear-sighted analysis of himself. Few persons have confided to us their observations in this kind with more winning candor. That is, when he sees fit. His "Autobiography" is not a psychological confession and deals intentionally with the external. But the glimpses of inner life that he does give have a singular clarity. He admitted his merits, if we may accept the account of Mr. Wilson, whose conversations with him generally bear the strongest mark of spiritual veracity. "You always do the right thing," said Mr. Wilson. "Well," said Jefferson modestly, "I believe I make fewer mistakes than most men. I think I am tactful rather than politic, the difference between which is very great." [44] I find this a little hard to swallow. But Jefferson's ample admission of his faults and weaknesses is apparent everywhere and is really charming. He agrees to accept a rôle to please a friend: "I did so, partly to help my old partner, and partly to see my name in large letters. This was the first time I had ever enjoyed that felicity, and it had a most soothing influence upon me." [45] He sees a rival actor and appreciates his excellence, "though I must confess that I had a hard struggle even inwardly to acknowledge it. As I look back and call to mind the slight touch of envy that I felt that night, I am afraid that I had hoped to see something not quite so good, and was a little annoyed to find him such a capital actor." [46] All actors and all men feel these things; not all have the honesty to say them.

Also, Jefferson's vivacity and activity of spirit made him widely conversant with many subjects. "I never discussed any topic of current interest or moment with him," says Colonel Watterson, "that he did not throw upon it the side-lights of a luminous understanding, and at the same time an impartial and intelligent judgment." [47] It must not be supposed, however, that he was a profound or systematic thinker, and his acquaintance with books, though fairly wide, was somewhat superficial. Even Shakespeare, whom he worshiped and introduced constantly into discussion and argument, he had never read through.

The truth is, he was too busy living to read. He relished life, in all its forms and energies. He was fond of sport, and entered into it with boyish ardor. His love of fishing is widely known, because it figured in his relation with President Cleveland. Their hearty comradeship is well illustrated by the pleasant anecdote of Cleveland's waiting impatiently while Jefferson chatted at his ease with the commander of the Oneida. "Are you going fishing or not?" called out the President in despair. "I do not mean to stir until I have finished my story to the Commodore," said the actor. [48] Jefferson sometimes shot as well as fished. But in later years the gun was too much for his natural tenderness. "I don't shoot any more," he said; "I can't bear to see the birds die." [49] And it is characteristic that to an interviewer, who had ventured some casual comment on the subject, he remarked later, "You said you didn't like to kill things! It made such an impression on me that I've never been shooting since." [50]

Jefferson would have been even more absorbed in

sport if he had not had another distraction which fascinated him and took most of the time and strength that he could spare from his regular pursuits. From his childhood he loved to paint. His father did a good deal of scene-painting and the son, hardly out of infancy, would get hold of the father's colors and busy himself with them for hours. The passion endured and grew, and Jefferson even felt that, if he had not been an actor, he would have been a painter and a successful one. His work, mostly landscapes, shows the grace, sensibility, and subtle imaginative quality of his temperament as well as the influence of the great French painters whom he so much admired.

But what interests us about Jefferson's painting is the hold it had upon him and the zeal with which he threw himself into it at all times. When he was at home, he shut himself into his studio and worked. When he was touring the country, and acting regularly, "in the early morning — at half-past six or so — he would be heard calling for his coffee and for his palette and brushes. It was very hard to get any conversation out of him during the day that did not in some way lead up to painting." [51] This is one of the curious cases of a man with a genius for one form of art, possessed with the desire to excel in another. When asked if it were true that he would rather paint than act, he replied it most emphatically was. [52] At any rate, there can be no question that painting filled his thoughts almost as much as acting. When he was in Paris, he says, "I painted pictures all day and dreamed of them all night." [53] He cherished the hope that after his death his paintings would be prized and sought for, and he fondly instanced Corot, whose work did not begin to sell till he was fifty.[54] A scene of natural beauty always translated itself for him into a picture. One day, when he had been admiring such a scene, a friend said to him, "Why don't you paint it?" "No, no, no! Not now." "And when?" "Oh, sometime in the future — when I have forgotten it." [55] But the most charming comment on this pictorial passion is the little dialogue between Cleveland and Jefferson on the morning after Cleveland was nominated for the second time. Jefferson was standing at a window at Gray Gables, looking out over the Bay. Cleveland put a hand on his shoulder. "Joe," he said, "aren't you going to congratulate me?" And Jefferson: "Ah, I do! Believe me, I do congratulate you. But, good God, if I could paint like *that*, you could be president of a dozen United States and I wouldn't change places with you." [56]

The drawback to painting, at least in Jefferson's case, was that it was a solitary pleasure. It was only when alone that artistic ideas would come to him.[57] He commented on this with his usual delicate wit. "But if I like to be alone when I paint, I have no objection to a great many people when I act." [58] And in general he had no objection to a great many people, liked them in fact, and was a thoroughly social and human being. He had all the qualities of a peculiarly social temperament. "He was full of caprices," says Winter; "mercurial and fanciful; a creature of moods; exceedingly, almost morbidly sensitive; eagerly desirous to please, because he loved to see people happy." [59]

He could enter into the happiness of others, and quite as keenly into their distress. He was "sensible of the misfortunes and sufferings of the lame, the blind, the deaf, and the wretched." [60] He not only felt these things and relieved them with words, with counsel, and with sympathy; but he was ready and active with deeds, both in the way of effort and in the way of money. With the shrewdness of a Franklin, he saw the subjective as well as the objective benefit of such action. "My boys sometimes get discouraged," he remarked, "and I say to them: 'Go out and do something for somebody. Go out and give something to anybody, if it's only a pair of woolen stockings to a poor old woman. It will take you away from yourselves and make you happy.'" [61] He was sometimes spoken of as over-careful in money matters. Certainly he was not careless or wasteful. He knew that common sense applies to giving as to other things, and he was not liable to the reproach implied in his comment on a fellow-actor: "It was said of him that he was generous to a fault; and I think he must have been, for he never paid his washerwoman." [62] Jefferson paid his own washerwoman, before he helped other people's.

In human traits of a less practical order he was even richer. In company he was cordial, gay, sympathetic, amusing. He was an admirable story-teller, acted his narrative as well as spoke it, apologized for repeating himself, as good story-tellers too often do not, but made old anecdotes seem new by the freshness of his invention in detail. He was tolerant of the talk of others, even of bores, even of impertinent interviewers, and all agree that he was an excellent listener. He knew that in our hurried, ignorant world those who listen are those who learn.

In the more intimate relations of life Jefferson's tenderness was always evident. He was twice married and had children by both wives and his family life was full of charm. I do not know that this can be better illustrated than by his daughter-in-law's story of his once enlarging upon the hideousness of the old idea of God as jealous and angry. This, he said, violated all the beauty of the true relation between parent and child. Whereupon one of his sons remarked, "You never taught us to be afraid of *you*, father." [63] Jefferson's affection for those who were gone seems to have had a peculiar tenacity and loyalty. Of his elder half-brother, Charles, especially, he always spoke with such vivid feeling that you felt that the memory was a clinging presence in his life.

His devotion to the friends who were with him in the flesh was equally sincere and attractive. The relation with the Clevelands naturally commands the most attention, and it is as creditable to one side as to the other. Jefferson understood perfectly his friend's great position in the world. He was absolutely indifferent to it, so far as the free, intimate commerce of daily intercourse went; yet never for one instant did he presume upon it for any purpose of self-exaltation or self-aggrandizement. I do not know where this is more delightfully illustrated than in the words of Gilder, the close friend of both men, writing to Mrs. Cleveland:

"I have just spent the night at Joseph Jefferson's; he was as angelic as ever, and speaks of yourself and the President always with that refinement of praise that honors the praised doubly — with that deep respect mingled with an affectionate tone, free of familiarity, that makes one feel like taking off one's hat whenever he says 'the President' or Mrs. 'Cleveland.' " [64]

The same sensibility that marks Jefferson's human relations shows in all his enjoyment of life. He liked pleasant things, pretty things. He was moderate in his eating, but he appreciated good food in good company. He liked to build houses and fill them with what was charming. He was too shrewd to be lavish, too shrewd to think that lavishness makes happiness. But he knew how to select the beautiful with delicacy and grace. He loved music, though here his taste was rather simple, and he quoted with relish "Bill" Nye's remark about Wagner, "My friend Wagner's music is really much better than it sounds." [65] He adored painting, studied it closely, and collected it as extensively as his means would allow, at times perhaps a little more so. His love for nature has already appeared with his painting. It was inexhaustible, and one of the best things Winter ever said about him was, "No other actor has expressed in art, as he did, the spirit of humanity in intimate relation with the spirit of physical nature." [66]

The sensitive and emotional quality that belonged to his aesthetic feeling was very evident in Jefferson's religious attitude. It does not appear that he had done any elaborate or systematic thinking upon such subjects and he did not trouble himself greatly with the external formalities of religion. "For sectarian creeds he entertained a profound contempt," says Winter, "and upon clergymen, as a class, he looked with distrust and aversion." [67] But he had an instinctive leaning toward a spiritual view of life. Immortality was not only a theory with him, but an actual, vivid fact; so that he seemed constantly to feel about him the presence of those whom he had lost. In this he resembled the Swedenborgians, to whose doctrines he was favorable, without perhaps knowing much about them. He carried his receptiveness for spiritual phenomena to the verge of credulity, at the same time always tingeing and correcting it with his wholesome humor and irony. Once he came into the company of Cleveland just as some other person present was telling something a little difficult for ordinary minds to swallow. "Ah," cried Cleveland, "tell that to Jefferson: he'll believe anything." And Jefferson answered, "Of course I will. The world is full of wonders, and another, more or less, does not surprise me." [68]

What is winning about Jefferson's religion is its cheerfulness, serenity, and love. To be as happy as possible one's self and especially to make others happy, was the cardinal doctrine of it, and I do not know that it can be improved upon. Above all, he was an enemy to fear. He told Miss Shaw "that everything that was detrimental either to the physical or the spiritual health of humanity had its origin in fear. And this he believed in casting out entirely. . . . He told me that he had labored for years with this end in view, believing that the conquering of fear would harmonize his character as much as it was possible for him to do." [69]

Evidently there was some struggle about this, and the interest of Jefferson's cheerfulness and optimism lies largely in the fact that they were not a matter of temperament, but a matter of will. His was not the easy-going, Bohemian carelessness, which takes fortune and misfortune with equal indifference. He liked joy and laughter and sought them and cultivated them. But he was sensitive and capable of suffering intensely. There was a strain of melancholy in him, all the more subtle for being controlled. When some one classed him as an optimist, he protested: "No — no, he is mistaken, I am not an optimist. I too often let things sadden me." [70] Ugliness he hated. Decay he hated. "I cannot endure destruction of any kind." [71] Old age he hated, never would admit that he was old, kept his heart youthful, at any rate. The secret of life, he knew, is looking forward, and he filled his spirit full of the things that look forward, to this life or another. Thus it was that he loved gardens and flowers. "The saddest thing in old age," he said to Mr. Wilson, "is the absence of expectation. You no longer look forward to things. Now a garden is all expectation" — here his thought took the humorous turn so characteristic of him — "and you often get a lot of things you don't expect." Then he returned to the serious. "Therefore I have become a gardener. My boy, when you are past seventy, don't forget to cultivate a garden. It is all expectation." [72]

JOSEPH JEFFERSON

This delightful blending of laughter and pathos, of tenderness and irony, coupled with Jefferson's constant association with the stage, makes one connect him irresistibly with the clowns of Shakespeare. Touchstone and Feste and the fool of Lear are not fools in the ordinary sense. Their keenness, their apprehension, their subtlety are often, in specific cases, much beyond those of common mortals. It is simply that they take with seriousness matters which the children of this world think trifling and see as trifles under the haunting aspect of eternity those solemn passions and efforts which grave human creatures regard as the important interests of life. With this airy, gracious, fantastic temper Jefferson had always something in common, however practical he might be when a compelling occasion called for it. He loved dolls, and toy-shops, would spend hours in them, watching the children and entering into their ecstasy. He would stand before the windows and put chatter into the dolls' mouths. "Look at that old fool taking up his time staring and laughing at us. I wonder if he thinks we have no feelings." "Isn't this a sloppy sort of day for dolls? Not even fit to look out of the window!" "Hello, Margery, who tore your skirt?" [73] Don't you hear Touchstone? Don't you hear Rip Van Winkle? "At New Orleans," he said to Mr. Wilson, "Eugene Field and I ranged through the curiosity shops, and the man would buy *dolls* and *such* things." And Wilson told him that "Field said he never saw a man like Jefferson — that his eye was caught with all sorts of gewgaws, and that he simply squandered money on trifles." And Jefferson chuckled, "That's it: one half the world thinks the other half crazy." [74]

So the solution and dissolution of all life, with its passion and effort and despair and hope, in quaint and tender laughter bring Jefferson fully into the company of the children of dream. Mark Twain, with his vast wandering, his quest of fortune, his touching of all men's hands and hearts, was a thing of dream, and confessed it. Emily Dickinson, shut off in her white Amherst solitude, daughter of thoughts and flowers, was a thing of dream, and knew it. With Jefferson the very nature of stage life made the dream even more insistent and pervading. And on the stage to act one part, over and over, till the identities of actor and acted were mingled inseparably! And to have that part Rip Van Winkle, a creature of dream, if ever human being was!

And Jefferson himself recognized this flavor of dream again and again. He liked the strange, the mysterious, the mystical, preferred to seek the explanation of natural things in supernatural causes. The actor's glory, so immense, so all-involving for a moment, does it not flit away into oblivion, like a bubble or a dream? Trifles all, toys all, diversions of dolls, and fit for dolls to play with! "Is *anything* worth while?" he said. "What, perhaps, does the best or worst any of us can do amount to in this vast conglomeration of revolving worlds? On the other hand, isn't *everything* worth while? Is not the smallest thing of importance?" [75] So he mocked and meditated, as Feste might have done in the gardens of Olivia, while Sir

Toby drank, and Viola and Orsino caressed and kissed.
He loved to sum up his own and all life in a phrase of
Seneca: "Life is like a play upon the stage; it signifies
not how long it lasts, but how well it is acted. Die when
or where you will, think only on making a good exit." [76]
But I am sure, if he had known them, he would have
preferred the magnificent lines with which Fitzgerald
ends his translation of the great dream play of Calderon:

> "Such a doubt
> Confounds and clouds our mortal life about.
> And, whether wake or dreaming, this I know,
> How dream-wise human glories come and go;
> Whose momentary tenure not to break,
> Walking as one who knows he soon may wake,
> So fairly carry the full cup, so well
> Disordered insolence and passion quell,
> That there be nothing after to upbraid
> Dreamer or doer in the part he played,
> Whether To-morrow's dawn shall break the spell,
> Or the Last Trumpet of the eternal Day,
> When Dreaming with the Night shall pass away."

NOTES

NOTES

THE notes to each chapter are preceded by a list of the most important works referred to, with the abbreviations used.

I: MARK TWAIN

Paine, Albert Bigelow, *Mark Twain; A Biography*,
  three volumes, paged continuously.   *Biography.*
Twain, Mark, *Letters*, arranged with comment by
  Albert Bigelow Paine, two volumes, paged continuously.   *Letters.*
Twain, Mark, *Works*, Hillcrest Edition, twenty-five
  volumes. (This edition is not complete, but is
  quoted for all writings contained in it.)   *Works.*

1. *Letters*, p. 128.
2. *Letters*, p. 643.
3. *Biography*, p. 241.
4. *Biography*, p. 146.
5. *Biography*, p. 109.
6. *Works*, vol. VI, p. 234.
7. *Letters*, p. 416.
8. *Biography*, p. 1328.
9. *Letters*, p. 734.
10. *Biography*, p. 1256.
11. *Biography*, p. 773.
12. *Letters*, p. 543.
13. *Works*, vol. V, p. 119.
14. Mark Twain, *Autobiography*, in *North American Review*,
    vol. CLXXXV, p. 121.
15. W. D. Howells, *My Mark Twain*, p. 178.
16. *Biography*, p. 844.
17. Mark Twain, *Autobiography*, in *North American Review*.
    vol. CLXXXV, p. 5.
18. *Biography*, p. 1366.
19. *Works*, vol. XIII, p. 279.
20. Mark Twain, *What is Man and Other Essays*, p. 75.
21. *Letters*, p. 337.

22. *Biography,* p. 1451.
23. *Letters,* p. 527.
24. Mark Twain, *Autobiography,* in *North American Review,* vol. CLXXXIII, p. 457.
25. *Letters,* p. 528.
26. Mark Twain, *Speeches,* p. 32.
27. Mark Twain, *Autobiography,* in *North American Review,* vol. CLXXXIII, p. 583.
28. Mark Twain, *The Mysterious Stranger,* p. 150.
29. *Biography,* p. 1292.

II: HENRY ADAMS

Adams, Henry, *The Education of Henry Adams; An Autobiography.*   *Education.*
Adams, Henry, *Mont-Saint-Michel and Chartres. Saint-Michel.*

1. *Education,* p. 314.
2. *Education,* p. 68.
3. *Education,* p. 9.
4. *Education,* p. 34.
5. *Education,* p. 64.
6. *Education,* p. 59.
7. *Education,* p. 66.
8. *Education,* p. 56.
9. *Education,* p. 65.
10. *Education,* p. 70.
11. *Education,* p. 76.
12. *Education,* p. 77.
13. *Education,* p. 78.
14. *Education,* p. 79.
15. *Education,* p. 75.
16. *Education,* p. 81.
17. Henry Cabot Lodge, *Early Memories,* p. 186.
18. *Education,* p. 300.
19. *Ibid.*
20. *Education,* p. 307.
21. William Roscoe Thayer, *The Life and Letters of John Hay,* vol. II, p. 55.
22. William Roscoe Thayer, *The Life and Letters of John Hay,* vol. II, p. 61.

NOTES

23. *Education*, p. 105.
24. *Education*, p. 118.
25. *Ibid.*
26. *Education*, p. 307.
27. *Education*, p. 85.
28. *Education*, p. 353.
29. *Saint-Michel*, p. 198.
30. *Education*, p. 443.
31. *Education*, p. 106.
32. *Education*, p. 108.
33. Henry Adams, *Letters to a Niece*, p. 4.
34. Henry Adams, *Letters to a Niece,* p. 16.
35. *Education*, p. 170.
36. *Education*, p. 175.
37. Preface to *A Letter to American Teachers of History*, in *The Degradation of the Democratic Dogma*, p. 138.
38. *Education*, p. 394.
39. *Education*, p. 90.
40. *Ibid.*
41. *Education*, p. 285.
42. *Education*, p. 351.
43. *Education*, p. 413.
44. *Education*, p. 357.
45. *Education*, p. 420.
46. *Education*, p. 220.
47. *Saint-Michel*, p. 213.
48. *Saint-Michel*, p. 178.
49. *Education*, p. 232.
50. *Education*, p. 68.
51. *Education*, p. 255.
52. *Education*, p. 369.
53. *Saint-Michel*, p. 9.
54. *Education*, p. 81.
55. *Letters to a Niece*, p. 18.
56. *Saint-Michel*, p. 166.
57. *Education*, p. 352.
58. *Education*, p. 424.
59. *Education*, p. 381.
60. *Saint-Michel*, p. 111.
61. *Education*, p. 95.

62. *Education*, p. 441.
63. Beth Bradford Gilchrist, *The Life of Mary Lyon*, p. 198.

III: SIDNEY LANIER

Lanier, Sidney, *Letters*. *Letters*.
Lanier, Sidney, *Poems* (edition 1900). *Poems*.
Mims, Edwin, *Sidney Lanier*. Mims.

1. *Letters*, p. 14 (condensed).
2. *Letters*, p. 114.
3. Mims, p. 153.
4. To Northrupp, June 11, 1866, in *Lippincott's Magazine*, vol. LXXV, p. 307.
5. Mims, p. 5.
6. Mims, p. 321.
7. *Letters*, p. 51.
8. *The Letters of Thomas Gray* (ed. Tovey), vol. I, p. 150.
9. *Letters*, p. 132.
10. Mims, p. 157.
11. Mims, p. 91.
12. *Letters*, p. 46.
13. *Ibid.*
14. Mims, p. 321.
15. Mims, p. 125.
16. *Poems*, p. xxii.
17. To Northrupp, July 28, 1866, in *Lippincott's Magazine*, vol. LXXV, p. 310.
18. *Letters*, p. 79.
19. *Letters*, p. 73.
20. Mims, p. 39.
21. Mims, p. 303.
22. Mims, p. 31.
23. *Letters*, p. 103.
24. *Ibid.*
25. Sidney Lanier, *Poem Outlines*, p. 18.
26. Mims, p. 96.
27. *Letters*, p. 154.
28. *Letters*, p. 77.
29. Sidney Lanier, *Retrospects and Prospects*, p. 5.
30. *Poems*, p. 143.

NOTES

31. Sidney Lanier, *Poem Outlines*, p. 104.
32. *Letters*, p. 168.
33. *Letters*, p. 194.
34. *Letters*, p. 13.
35. *Letters*, p. 226.
36. *Letters*, p. 50.
37. Mims, p. 6.
38. *Letters*, p. 107.
39. Mims, p. 310.
40. *Letters*, p. 184.
41. Mims, p. 35.
42. *Letters*, p. 171.
43. Mims, p. 66.
44. *Letters*, p. 71.
45. *Letters*, p. 84.
46. *Letters*, p. 133.
47. Mims, p. 308.
48. *Letters*, p. 224.
49. *Letters*, p. 106.
50. *Ibid.*
51. *Letters*, p. 109.
52. *Letters*, p. 68.
53. Mims, p. 330.
54. Mims, p. 145.
55. *Letters*, p. 66.
56. *Letters*, p. 238.
57. *Poems*, p. 31.
58. *Letters*, p. 78.
59. *Poems*, p. 246.

IV: JAMES McNEILL WHISTLER

Menpes, Mortimer, *Whistler as I Knew Him.*   Menpes.
Pennell, E. R. and J., *The Life of James McNeill*
    Whistler, sixth edition, revised.   Pennell.
Seitz, Don Carlos, *Whistler Stories.*   Seitz.
Whistler, James McNeill, *The Gentle Art of Making*
    Enemies.   *Gentle Art.*

1. Seitz, p. 27.
2. Seitz, p. 70.

3. Menpes, p. 63.
4. Pennell, p. 358.
5. Pennell, p. 412.
6. *Gentle Art*, p. 29.
7. Pennell, p. 404.
8. Pennell, p. 138.
9. Frederick Keppel, *One Day with Whistler*, p. 8.
10. Menpes, p. 8.
11. Pennell, p. 323.
12. Menpes, p. 7.
13. Gilbert K. Chesterton, *Heretics*, p. 244.
14. Menpes, p. 140.
15. Menpes, p. 43.
16. Menpes, p. 38.
17. Pennell, p. 343.
18. Otto H. Bacher, *With Whistler in Venice*, p. 157.
19. Chris Healy, *Confessions of a Journalist*, p. 203.
20. Pennell, p. 237.
21. *Trilby*, in *Harper's New Monthly Magazine*, vol. LXXXVIII, p. 577.
22. Pennell, p. 211.
23. Menpes, p. 132.
24. Pennell, p. 366.
25. Seitz, p. 73.
26. John C. Van Dyke, *American Painting and Its Tradition*, p. 173.
27. Alexander Harrison quoted by Frank Harris, *Contemporary Portraits*, p. 80.
28. Pennell, p. 105.
29. Menpes, p. 37.
30. Pennell, p. 205. So in first edition, somewhat altered in sixth.
31. Menpes, p. 10.
32. Menpes, p. 33.
33. Pennell, p. 104.
34. Pennell, p. 119.
35. Pennell, p. 323.
36. Menpes, p. 117.
37. John C. Van Dyke, *American Painting and Its Tradition*, p. 173.

38. Seitz, p. 33.
39. Seitz, p. 45.
40. *Gentle Art*, p. 115.
41. Pennell, p. 409.
42. Sir Walter Raleigh, *Speech at Opening of Whistler Memorial Exhibition*, p. 10.
43. Menpes, p. 10.
44. Pennell, p. 285.
45. Pennell, p. 422.
46. Pennell, p. 300.
47. Pennell, p. 277.
48. T. Martin Wood, *Whistler*, p. 20.
49. Pennell, p. 117.
50. J. K. Huysmans, *Certains*, p. 69.
51. Pennell, p. 222.
52. Seitz, p. 119.
53. Pennell, p. 284.
54. Pennell, p. 402.
55. Seitz, p. 120.

V: JAMES GILLESPIE BLAINE

Blaine, Mrs. James G., *Letters*, edited by Harriet S. Blaine Beale, two volumes.   Mrs. Blaine.
Conwell, R. H., *The Life and Public Services of James G. Blaine.*   Conwell.
Hamilton, Gail, *Biography of James G. Blaine.*   Hamilton.
Stanwood, Edward, *James Gillespie Blaine.*   Stanwood.
The letters to Warren Fisher, Jr., are printed in full in *Mr. Blaine's Record: The Investigation of 1876 and The Mulligan Letters, Published by the Committee of One Hundred.* (Boston.)

1. Mrs. Blaine, vol. II, p. 214.
2. Hamilton, p. 492.
3. Mrs. Blaine, vol. II, p. 218.
4. Mrs. Blaine, vol. I, p. 136.
5. Hamilton, p. 469.
6. Hamilton, p. 301.
7. Conwell, p. 392.
8. Conwell, p. 89.

9. Hamilton, p. 620.
10. Mrs. Blaine, vol. I, p. 303.
11. Hamilton, p. 532.
12. Mrs. Blaine, vol. II, p. 36.
13. Mrs. Blaine, vol. II, p. 121.
14. Mrs. Blaine, vol. II, p. 135.
15. Mrs. Blaine, vol. II, p. 183.
16. Mrs. Blaine, vol. II, p. 185. Sentences transposed.
17. Mrs. Blaine, vol. II, p. 220.
18. Mrs. Blaine, vol. II, p. 131.
19. Mrs. Blaine, vol. II, p. 16.
20. Mrs. Blaine, vol. I, p. 191.
21. Hamilton, p. 455.
22. Hamilton, p. 225.
23. Hamilton, p. 245.
24. Hamilton, p. 467.
25. Hamilton, p. 300.
26. Mrs. Blaine, vol. I, p. 185.
27 Hamilton, p. 536.
28. George F. Hoar, *Autobiography of Seventy Years*, vol. I, p. 378.
29. Andrew Dickson White, *Autobiography*, vol. I, p. 214.
30 George F. Hoar, *Autobiography of Seventy Years*, vol. I, p. 200.
31 Hamilton, p. 707.
32 Stanwood, p. 109.
33. James Ford Rhodes, *History of the United States from Hayes to McKinley*, p. 321.
34. Mrs. Blaine, vol. I, p. 292.
35. Conwell, p. 67.
36. Conwell, p. 86.
37. Hamilton, p. 436.
38. A neighbor of Blaine's, in Conwell, p. 87.
39. Hamilton, p. 107.
40. Hamilton, p. 581.
41. Hamilton, p. 147.
42. George F. Hoar, *Autobiography of Seventy Years*, vol. I, p. 200.
43. Mrs. Blaine, vol. I, p. 137.
44. Stanwood, p. 361.

NOTES

45. Hamilton, p. 633.
46. Note in Mrs. Blaine, vol. ii, p. 13.
47. Mrs. Blaine, vol. i, p. 277.
48. Hamilton, p. 477.
49. Mrs. Blaine, vol. i, p. 72.
50. Mrs. Blaine, vol. i, p. 159.
51. To Fisher, October 1, 1871.
52. To Fisher, August 9, 1872.
53. To Fisher, October 4, 1869.
54. To Fisher, June 29, 1869.
55. Fisher to Blaine, April 16, 1872.
56. Stanwood, p. 162.
57. Enclosure in Blaine to Fisher, April 16, 1876.
58. Speech of April 24, 1876. In *Congressional Record*, Forty Fourth Congress, 1st Session, vol. iv, part 3, p. 2725.
59. Hamilton, p. 395.
60. James Russell Lowell, *Letters*, vol. ii, p. 170.
61. James Ford Rhodes, *History of the United States from the Compromise of 1850*, vol. vii, p. 205.
62. George F. Hoar, *Autobiography of Seventy Years*, vol. i, p. 281.
63. Hamilton, p. 432.
64. *Congressional Record*, June 5, 1876, Forty-Fourth Congress, 1st Session, vol. iv, part 4, p. 3606.
65. Hamilton, p. 424.
66. Hamilton, p. 536.
67. Stanwood, p. 342.
68. James G. Blaine, *Political Discussions*, p. 465.
69. Mrs. Blaine, vol. ii, p. 120. For a curious discussion of the attitude of Mrs. Blaine toward the possibility of her husband's nomination in a later campaign see *These Shifting Scenes*, by Charles Edward Russell, chapter vii.

VI: GROVER CLEVELAND

Black, Chauncey F., *The Lives of Grover Cleveland and Thomas A. Hendricks.*   Black.

Cleveland, Grover, *Fishing and Shooting Sketches.*   *Fishing Sketches.*

Cleveland, Grover, *The Writings and Speeches*

of Grover Cleveland, Selected and edited by
George F. Parker.   *Writings.*
Gilder, Richard Watson, *Grover Cleveland; A
Record of Friendship.*   Gilder.
Parker, George F., *Recollections of Grover Cleve-
land.*   Parker.
West, Andrew F., article in *Century*, volume
LXXVII, January, 1909, *Grover Cleveland: A
Princeton Memory.*   West.
Williams, Jesse Lynch Williams, *Mr. Cleve-
land, A Personal Impression.*   Williams.

1. Henry Watterson, "*Marse Henry*," an *Autobiography*, vol.
   II, p. 118.
2. *Writings*, p. 338.
3. Parker, p. 391.
4. Black, p. 43.
5. *Fishing Sketches*, p. 45.
6. Gilder, p. 171.
7. West, p. 328.
8. West, p. 326.
9. Black, p. 63.
10. Parker, p. 382.
11. Gilder, p. 48.
12. Gilder, p. 249.
13. Williams, pp. 24, 25.
14. West, p. 336.
15. *Fishing Sketches*, p. 53.
16. James Russell Lowell, *Letters*, vol. II, p. 326.
17. Gilder, p. 192.
18. Parker, p. 377.
19. Williams, p. 61.
20. Speech to Grover Cleveland Association in New York,
    March 18, 1919, in *Boston Transcript*, March 19,
    1919.
21. *Fishing Sketches*, p. 13.
22. James Shirley, *The Bird in a Cage*, act IV, scene 1.
23. For this story I am indebted to my wife, who observed
    the incident.
24. Gilder, p. 47.

NOTES

25. Frederick E. Goodrich, *The Life and Public Services of Grover Cleveland*, p. 74.
26. *Ibid.*
27. Gilder, p. 259.
28. *Writings*, p. 534.
29. Leonard Wood, in Speech to Grover Cleveland Association in New York, March 18, 1919, in *Boston Transcript*, March 19, 1919.
30. Williams, p. 11.
31. *Writings*, p. 212.
32. James D. Richardson, *Messages and Papers of the Presidents*, vol. VIII, p. 450.
33. *Fishing Sketches*, p. 28.
34. *Fishing Sketches*, p. 30.
35. Gilder, p. 36.
36. Williams, p. 31.
37. Gilder, p. 30.
38. *Fishing Sketches*, p. 106.
39. Gilder, p. 49.
40. James Russell Lowell, *Letters*, vol. II, p. 344.
41. Black, p. 61.
42. Gilder, p. 169.
43. Parker, p. 35.
44. Parker, p. 341.
45. *Writings*, p. 264.
46. Parker, p. 210.
47. Parker, p. 335.
48. *Messages from the Governors of the State of New York*, edited by Charles Z. Lincoln, vol. VII, p. 873.
49. Gilder, p. 30.
50. See Life of General E. S. Bragg, supposedly supplied by himself, in *Who's Who in America* for 1902.
51. Henry Watterson, "*Marse Henry*," *an Autobiography*, vol. II, p. 144.
52. Henry Adams, *The Education of Henry Adams*, p. 320.
53. To E. P. Wheeler, printed in *Sixty Years of American Life*, by Everett P. Wheeler, p. 250.
54. For the history of this expression as finally shaped by Colonel Lamont see Parker, pp. 43, 44.
55. Gail Hamilton, *Biography of James G. Blaine*, p. 515.

56. *Writings*, p. 86.
57. *Fishing Sketches*, p. 87.
58. Parker, p. 349.
59. Parker, p. 105.
60. James D. Richardson, *Messages and Papers of the Presidents*, vol. VIII, p. iv.
61. Gilder, p. 191.
62. West, p. 336.
63. Gilder, p. 190.
64. Gilder, p. 179.
65. Gilder, p. 270.

VII: HENRY JAMES

James, Henry, *Letters*, Selected and edited by Percy Lubbock, two volumes.   *Letters.*
James, Henry, *The Novels and Tales of Henry James*, Charles Scribner's Sons, twenty-six volumes. (This edition, with prefaces and extensive revision by the author, does not comprise all of James's works, but is quoted for all writings contained in it.)   *Works.*
James, Henry, *Notes of a Son and Brother.*   *Son and Brother.*
James, Henry, *A Small Boy and Others.*   *Small Boy.*

1. *Letters*, vol. I, p. 165.
2. Henry James, *The Art of Fiction* (printed with an essay by Walter Besant on the same subject), p. 66. Also in *Partial Portraits*, by Henry James, p. 390.
3. *Letters*, vol. II, p. 489.
4. *Works*, vol. XXIV, p. 349.
5. *Works*, vol. XXI, p. xxi.
6. *Works*, vol. XII, p. ix.
7. *Small Boy*, p. 263.
8. *Works*, vol. V, p. viii.
9. *Irish Essays* (edition 1882), p. v.
10. *Letters*, vol. II, p. 347.
11. *Works*, vol. IX, p. v.
12. *Letters*, vol. I, p. 289.
13. *Letters*, vol. II, p. 490.
14. *Works*, vol. IX, p. 303.

NOTES

15. *Works*, vol. xviii, p. 422.
16. *Letters*, vol. ii, p. 119.
17. *Works*, vol. xxi, p. v.
18. *Letters*, vol. ii, p. 323.
19. *Letters*, vol. ii, p. 9.
20. William James, *Letters*, vol. i, p. 41.
21. *Letters*, vol. ii, p. 11.
22. Theodora Bosanquet, in *Yale Review*, vol. x, p. 156.
23. *Letters*, vol. i, p. 310.
24. *Letters*, vol. i, p. 309.
25. *Letters*, vol. i, p. 101.
26. *Letters*, vol. i, p. 115.
27. *Letters*, vol. i, p. 337.
28. Henry James, *French Poets and Novelists* (English edition, 1878), p. 109.
29. *Ibid.*
30. Henry James, *The American Scene* (American edition, 1907), p. 367.
31. Henry James, *French Poets and Novelists*, p. 175.
32. *Letters*, vol. i, p. 379.
33. Lawrence Pearsall Jacks, *Life and Letters of Stopford Brooke*, vol. ii, p. 672.
34. *Letters*, vol. i, p. 348. A correspondent writes me that James's brother Wilkie, commenting upon Henry's imperfect knowledge of women, declared that he "had never been in love, and lacked the insight which that experience gave to a man." Such a general negative as this is somewhat difficult to accept, but it is exceedingly suggestive.
35. *Son and Brother*, p. 324.
36. *Letters*, vol. i, p. 183.
37. *Letters*, vol. ii, p. 104.
38. *Works*, vol. xv, p. 22.
39. *Works*, vol. v, p. xxi.
40. *Letters*, vol. i, p. 198.
41. *Letters*, vol. ii, p. 102.
42. *Letters*, vol. i, p. 68.
43. *Works*, vol. ix, p. xxiii.
44. *Letters*, vol. i, p. 103.
45. *Works*, vol. x, p. x.
46. *Letters*, vol. i, p. 409.

47. *Works*, vol. x, p. xi.
48. *Letters*, vol. i, p. 180.
49. *Letters*, vol. i, p. 173.
50. *Letters*, vol. i, p. 182.
51. Henry James, *French Poets and Novelists*, p. 400.
52. *Letters*, vol. ii, p. 485.

VIII: JOSEPH JEFFERSON

Jefferson, Eugénie Paul, *Intimate Recollections of Joseph Jefferson.*	Mrs. Jefferson.
Jefferson, Joseph, *The Autobiography of Joseph Jefferson.*	*Autobiography.*
Wilson, Francis, *Joseph Jefferson.*	Wilson.
Winter, William, *Life and Art of Joseph Jefferson.*	Winter, *Life.*
Winter, William, *Other Days.*	*Other Days.*

1. Winter, *Life*, p. 136.
2. *Autobiography*, p. 115.
3. Winter, *Life*, p. 15.
4. *Other Days*, p. 88.
5. Mrs. Jefferson, p. 204.
6. Henry Watterson, "*Marse Henry*," An *Autobiography*, vol. ii, p. 183.
7. Winter, *Life*, p. 168.
8. William Winter, *Life and Art of Edwin Booth* (edition, 1894), p. 107.
9. Mary Shaw, in *Century*, vol. lxxxiii, p. 736.
10. Wilson, p. 330.
11. *Autobiography*, p. 439.
12. Wilson, p. 28.
13. *Autobiography*, p. 23.
14. *Autobiography*, p. 101.
15. *Autobiography*, p. 303.
16. *Other Days*, p. 81.
17. *Autobiography*, p. 118.
18. *Autobiography*, p. 101.
19. *Autobiography*, p. 340.
20. Mary Shaw, in *Century*, vol. lxxxiii, p. 731.

NOTES

21. Henry Watterson, "*Marse Henry*," *An Autobiography*, vol. II, p. 185.
22. Mary Shaw, in *Century*, vol. LXXXV, p. 382.
23. Mary Shaw, in *Century*, vol. LXXXIII, p. 732.
24. *Autobiography*, p. 402.
25. Winter, *Life*, p. 195.
26. *Other Days*, p. 86.
27. Mary Shaw, in *Century*, vol. LXXXIII, p. 735.
28. *Autobiography*, p. 222.
29. Wilson, p. 172.
30. *Autobiography*, p. 132.
31. *Autobiography*, p. 303.
32. Wilson, p. 128.
33. *Autobiography*, p. 115.
34. Wilson, p. 11.
35. Wilson, p. 8.
36. Mary Shaw, in *Century*, vol. LXXXIII, p. 736.
37. *Rip Van Winkle as Played by Joseph Jefferson*, p. 171.
38. Wilson, p. 68.
39. *Autobiography*, p. 158.
40. Mrs. Jefferson, p. 169. From an interview reported in the *New York Herald*.
41. *Ibid.*
42. *Autobiography*, pp. 224–229 and 302–310.
43. *Other Days*, p. 75.
44. Wilson, p. 25.
45. *Autobiography*, p. 116.
46. *Autobiography*, p. 81.
47. Henry Watterson, "*Marse Henry*," *An Autobiography*, vol. II, p. 173.
48. Wilson, p. 59.
49. Mrs. Jefferson, p. 66.
50. Mrs. Jefferson, p. 70.
51. Mary Shaw, in *Century*, vol. LXXXIII, p. 735.
52. Wilson, p. 66.
53. *Autobiography*, p. 348.
54. Wilson, p. 84.
55. Wilson, p. 307, slightly abbreviated.
56. Eugénie Paul Jefferson, in *Outing*, vol. LIII, p. 739.
57. Wilson, p. 306.

58. *Ibid.*
59. *Other Days*, p. 86.
60. *Other Days*, p. 87.
61. Wilson, epigraph of book.
62. *Autobiography*, p. 216.
63. Mrs. Jefferson, p. 216.
64. Richard Watson Gilder, *Letters*, p. 162.
65. Wilson, p. 214.
66. *Other Days*, p. 78.
67. *Other Days*, p. 86.
68. *Other Days*, p. 78.
69. Mary Shaw, in *Century*, vol. LXXXV, p. 381.
70. Mrs. Jefferson, p. 211.
71. *Autobiography*, p. 381.
72. Wilson, p. 341.
73. Wilson, p. 13.
74. Wilson, p. 244.
75. Wilson, p. 321.
76. *Autobiography*, p. 474.

INDEX

INDEX

Adams, Henry, 69, 71, 112, 154; Chronology, 30; never educated, 31, 32; his idea of the object of education, 31; his definition of a teacher, 32, 33; a student at Harvard, 33; in Germany, 34, 35; a teacher at Harvard, 35, 36; his *salon* in Washington, 37; his general human relations, 37, 38; fared better with women than with men, 38, 39; his friendships, 39, 40; his marriage, 40; in London during the Civil War, 41, 42; his political experience in America, 42, 43; a true conservative, 42, 44; his view of the workings of American government, 43; traveled extensively, 43–45; gained little from art, 45, 46, 53; *Mont-Saint-Michel and Chartres*, 46; his interest in Darwinism, 47, 48, 50; lacked lucidity, 48–50; his theory of acceleration, 49; a Darwinian for fun, 50; as an author, 51, 53; lacked seriousness, 51; had little enthusiasm, 52, 53; his attitude toward religion, 54; inherited too much egotism, 54, 55; mistrusted simplicity, 56; needed to be de-educated, 56; on Presidents Harrison and Cleveland, 164.

Aldrich, Nelson W., 120.

Arnold, Matthew, 177.

Bacher, Otto H., on Whistler, 93.

Balzac, Honoré, 176, 185.

Barker, Dr., 119.

Birrell, Augustine, on Mark Twain, 23, 24.

Blaine, Emmons, 120.

Blaine, James Gillespie, 167; Chronology, 114; as seen by his wife,

115, 116, 119–21; his whole life political, 116; intensely active intellectually, 116, 117; a master of words, 117, 135; his religion, 118; cared little for art, 118, 119; his sensibility profound, 119; morbid about his health, 119, 120; devoted to his wife and children, 121–23; his social qualities, 123, 124; a consummate politician, 124, 128; his personal charm, 125; his remarkable memory, 126, 127; a magnetic man, 127; a natural leader, 127, 128; his statesmanship, 128–30; his financial career, 130–38; congressional investigation, 134, 135; his fundamental error, 137; his ambition for the presidency, 138–40.

Blaine, Mrs. J. G., her letters quoted, 115, 116, 117, 118, 120, 121, 123, 128, 130, 131, 140.

Bosanquet, Miss, Henry James's secretary, 183, 184.

Boston, solved the universe, 33.

Boucicault, Dion, 211.

Bourget, Paul, 179.

Bragg, Gen. E. S., 164.

Browning, Robert, 179.

Burchard, Rev. Samuel D., 139.

Burlingame, Anson, 127.

Burton, Lady, and Whistler, 90.

Calderon, Pedro, 223.

Carlisle, John G., 170.

Cellini, Benvenuto, Whistler compared to, 94.

Chesterfield, Lord, 126.

Chesterton, G. K., on Whistler, 94, 97, 101.

Cibber, Colley, a saying of Dr. Johnson about, 99.

245

INDEX

Clemens, Samuel Langhorne, *see*
Twain, Mark.
Cleveland, Stephen Grover, Chronology, 144; his early life, 145, 148,
150; earnestly devoted to his task,
146; nominated for the presidency,
147; lacking in cultivation, 148;
his manner of writing, 149; his
spiritual and religious attitude,
150, 151, 169; indifferent to art,
151; an ardent fisherman and
hunter, 152, 153; loved children,
153, 154; *Fishing and Shooting
Sketches*, quoted, 154, 158; simple
and frugal, 154, 155; very generous, 155; his friendship and personal affection, 156, 157; his humor, 157, 158, 160; unpopular,
159; had great public merits, 160;
thoroughly democratic, 160, 161;
his speeches, 161; had superb
physical strength, 162; an intense
party man, 162, 163; his enemies,
164; what he stands for in American history, 165–70; essentially a
conservative, 166; his *Presidential
Problems*, 167; the strong features
of his character, 167, 168; his use
of the veto power, 168, 169; his
passionate Americanism, 169, 170;
on Joseph Jefferson, 200; friendship
with Jefferson, 213, 215, 217, 219.
Cleveland, Mrs. Grover, 115, 155,
217, 218.
Committee of One Hundred, on
Blaine, 136.
Corot, Jean Baptiste, 215.
Cowper, William, quoted, 111.

Delane, John T., and Henry Adams,
41, 42.
Democratic party, principles of, 166.
Dickinson, Emily, 222.
Dream, the element of, in Mark
Twain, 7, 9–11, 13; in Joseph Jefferson, 222; in Emily Dickinson,
222.
Du Maurier, George, 97.

Eden, Sir William, and Whistler,
95, 98.
Elkins, Stephen B., 140.

Farnsworth, General, 147.
Field, Eugene, and Joseph Jefferson,
221.
Finn, Huck, 15, 16.
Fisher, Warren, Jr., and J. G. Blaine,
132–34, 138, 139.
Fitzgerald, Edward, quoted, 223.
Flaubert, Gustave, 78, 81.
Fletcher, Phineas, quoted, 78.
Franklin, Benjamin, 20.
Friends, born, not made, 39.

Garfield, President James A., 167;
Blaine's eulogy on, 117, 119.
Garibaldi, Giuseppe, 56.
Gautier, Théophile, 112.
Gay, Walter, on Whistler at work,
103.
Gentle Art of Making Enemies, The,
96, 99, 100.
German teaching, Henry Adams's
opinion of, 35.
Gilder, Richard Watson, 156, 217.
God, Mark Twain's idea of, 25, 26;
his place in the education of
Henry Adams, 54; Whistler's feeling about, 90.
Gray, Thomas, on money, 63, 64.

Haden, Sir Seymour, 95, 96.
Harrison, President Benjamin, 164.
Harvard College, "a good school,"
33; education at, 36, 38.
Hay, John, and Henry Adams, 39;
on Blaine, 125.
Heine, Heinrich, 95.
Hiscock, Frank, 120.
History of the United States, Henry
Adams's, 51.
Hoar, Senator George F., on Blaine,
117, 124, 128, 130, 137.
Howells, William Dean, 182; on
Mark Twain, 14.
Huysmans, J. K., on Whistler, 108.

246

INDEX

INDEX

Lucretius, Lanier compared to, 69, 70, 81, 82.
Lyon, Mary, 56, 57.

Macbeth, Lady, 116.
McKinley, President William, 157, 164.
Matthews, Charles J., 206.
Menpes, Mortimer, on Whistler, 89, 93, 94, 101, 103.
Meux, Lady, and Whistler, 98.
Milnes, Richard Monckton, and Henry Adams, 41.
Milton, John, 94; on fame, 78.
Mont-Saint-Michel and Chartres, by Henry Adams, 46, 49, 54.
Moore, George, 95, 96.
More, Hannah, 209.
Mulligan, James, 134.
Music, the art of struggle, 72; depends on human emotion, 107, 110.

Nye, "Bill," 218.

Old Times on the Mississippi, 3.

Raphael, his friendly courtesy, 100.
Republican party, principles of, 166.
Rhodes, James Ford, 137.
Richardson, James D., 168.
Rip Van Winkle, 207, 210, 211.
Root, Elihu, on Blaine, 129.
Roughing It, 3.

Saint Ives, 95.
Schumann, Robert, Lanier's criticism of, 68, 69.
Seneca, quoted, 223.
Seward, William H., 126, 129, 162.
Shakespeare, William, his clowns, 221, 222.
Shaw, Mary, and Joseph Jefferson, 202, 207, 209, 219.
Sherman, Gen. W. T., on Blaine, 129.
Speculation, two times when a man should not venture on, 7.

Stanwood, Edward, 139.
Stevenson, Robert Louis, 22.
Sumner, Charles, 34.
Swift, Jonathan, 97.

Teacher, Henry Adams's definition of a, 32, 33; affects eternity, 36.
Ten O'Clock, Whistler's, 90, 91.
Thought, carnivorous, 69.
Tilden, Samuel J., 162.
Trollope, Anthony, 176.
Twain, Mark, 69, 112, 222; Chronology, 2; not to be judged by ordinary standards, 3; his way of working, 4; liked literary glory, 4, 10; something of the bard about him, 4; essentially a journalist, 5; his early days, 5–7; walked the city roofs with Artemus Ward, 6; his energy, 6; followed his fancies, 6; wanted money for what it brings, 7, 9; loved to take a chance, 7, 9; a dreamer, 7, 9, 10, 13; never settled down, 7; had perfect health, 8; made friends of all sorts and conditions of men, 8; his love and tenderness, 8, 15, 21; never a good calculator, 9; tragedy and disaster, 10, 11; generally known as a laugher, 11, 12; was he a great humorist, 12, 13, 19; as a thinker, 13, 14, 16–18; his confessions, 15, 20; scrupulous in financial relations, 15; had a trained Presbyterian conscience, 15; trusted men, 16; lacked great spiritual resources, 18; thoroughly American, 19–21; his appearance, 20; democratic, 21, 22; his best-known books, 22; his influence on the masses, 23, 24; an overthrower of shams, 23, 24; compared to Voltaire, 24, 27; called a demolisher of reverence, 24–26; his idea of God, 25, 26; charged with evil influence, 26, 27; taken seriously, he is desolating, 27, 28; his visit to Whistler, 98.

INDEX